LONDON TRANSPORT
AT WAR

by

CHARLES GRAVES

OLDCASTLE BOOKS·ENGLAND
LONDON TRANSPORT MUSEUM

CONTENTS

Photographs by: *H.M. Ministry of Aircraft Production, Coventry Evening Telegraph, Fox Photos, Keystone Press Agency, Illustrated, London News Agency Photos, Mirror Features, New York Times, Planet News, Sport & General Press Agency, C. O. Thomas, Time & Life, Topical Press Agency*

1989

Oldcastle Books
18 Coleswood Road
Harpenden, Herts AL5 1EQ

Copyright © 1989 London Transport Museum

First published 1947 as London Transport Carried On

Published in association with the London Transport Museum

British Library Cataloguing in Publishing record available

ISBN 0 948353 56 2

9 8 7 6 5 4 3 2 1

Printed in Great Britain by BPCC Wheatons Ltd, Exeter

At 11.15am on 3rd September 1939, households all over Britain tuned in their wireless sets for a broadcast from the Prime Minister, Neville Chamberlain. He began with these now famous words: *'I am speaking to you from the Cabinet Room at No. 10 Downing Street. This morning, the British Ambassador in Berlin handed the German government a final note, stating that unless the British government heard from them by 11 o'clock that they were prepared at once to withdraw their troops from Poland, a state of war would exist between us. I have to tell you now that no such undertaking has been received, and that consequently this country is at war with Germany.'*

The announcement came as no surprise. War with Nazi Germany as a result of Hitler's aggression towards neighbouring countries had seemed increasingly likely for months. Exactly a year earlier, during the Munich Crisis, hostilities had been averted at the last moment by Chamberlain's 'piece of paper' agreement with Hitler, but it soon became clear that this had only postponed the inevitable conflict. The borrowed time did at least allow some preparations to be taken against the expected aerial bombardment by the Luftwaffe. London Transport, like most large organisations, had followed government instructions and appointed an Air Raid Precautions Committee as early as 1937. By September 1938, when the Munich Crisis arose, the Board had drawn up detailed defence plans which would allow the system to remain operational under aerial attack, with the safety of passengers and staff secured as far as possible. A year later, ARP arrangements came into effect on Friday 1st September, two days before the official declaration of war.

The first major task for London Transport was to assist in the mass evacuation of London's children, hospital patients and expectant mothers to the safety of the country. Nearly 13,000 evacuees were ferried to Waterloo alone by bus, tram and tube for transfer on to main line trains. In other cases the Board's buses and coaches were used for the whole journey and many drivers had no sleep for 36 hours. A national Railway Executive Committee came into being to oversee the operation of both the LPTB and the main line railways, though the existing management continued. Blackout restrictions were applied immediately, and London Transport's petrol and oil supplies were cut by 25 per cent as an economy measure. Bus services were heavily restricted or withdrawn altogether to save fuel and limit black-out working, and within four months more than 800 central area buses were lying idle. Some Green Line coach services, all of which had been withdrawn on 1st September, were being restored by this time, although they were to be cut out again in 1942. Underground, trolleybus and tram services also had to be reduced, but fortunately there was a considerable reduction in passenger demand because of the effect of the war on business and the evacuation of many offices.

More than half the modernisation and improvement work scheduled under the 1935–40 programme had been carried out by the autumn of 1939. Some of it continued during the first year of the war, though at a reduced level. The last tram to trolleybus conversion, in the Poplar area, was completed in June 1940 and some work on the Northern Line extension went on until the following year, but most new tasks undertaken by London Transport's engineers from 1939 onwards were directly concerned with the war. Tube stations in the central area, and the tunnels under the Thames, were protected against flooding in the event of the river, sewers or water mains being breached after bombing by the installation of floodgates and watertight doors. Disused platforms and passageways at a number of central Piccadilly Line stations were converted into emergency headquarters offices for the Board and the Railway Executive Committee, one of which was later used for meetings of the War Cabinet during the Blitz. Operations rooms for London's Anti-Aircraft Command were also established deep in a tube station within a few feet of the passing trains.

London Transport staff had been receiving regular ARP training in rescue, fire fighting and first aid since before the war, but in May 1940 the Board also formed its own Home Guard unit, which eventually had nearly 30,000 members. As growing numbers of male staff were called up for service in the Forces, the Board began to recruit more female staff to replace them. Women enthusiastically took on virtually every job previously reserved for men, including labouring and heavy engineering work, though they were not allowed to become drivers.

The long-expected air raids finally began in the summer of 1940. The first bombs to damage London Transport equipment hit New Malden on 16th August, and immediately demonstrated the vulnerability of the trolleybus system to aerial attack by bringing down a section of the overhead. Heavy bombing started on 7th September with a daylight raid on the Docks and East End. London was then bombed every night until 2nd November, after which the Blitz continued intermittently until May 1941. In 57 raids the Luftwaffe dropped some 13,500 tons of high explosive and incendiary bombs, killing more than 15,000 civilians. For every person killed, another 35 were made homeless.

The damage and disruption to the London Transport system were severe, but never crippling. A service of some kind could nearly always be maintained, though this was more difficult with the trams and the Underground when trackwork and tunnels were hit. Buses could always be diverted, and this was even possible with trolleybuses. Wherever necessary, maintenance crews erected new traction poles and overhead quickly and efficiently, often working on their tower wagons while the Blitz raged around them. The average time taken to reinstate the trolleybus service after an 'incident' was only four hours.

As soon as the Blitz started, thousands of Londoners took to the tubes for shelter. At first this was not officially encouraged, and as no special facilities had been installed or arrangements made, there were chaotic scenes. Mass Observation, the social study organisation, reported that *'for the first time in many hundreds of years civilised families conducted the whole of their leisure and domestic lives in full view of each other. . . . Most of these people were not merely sheltering in the tubes; they were living there'*. In the newly completed Central Line extension tunnels east of Liverpool Street, where trains were not yet running, there was no compulsion for shelterers to leave during the day, and many stayed down for weeks on end. Gradually sheltering facilities became properly organised with special admission tickets, bunk beds, refreshments and, at some stations, libraries, music and live entertainment. At one there was even a newspaper, *The Swiss Cottager*, produced by the local shelterers' committee. The Underground tunnels were not entirely safe from attack, however, and shelterers were killed in six separate bomb incidents when tube stations were hit. On Government instructions, London Transport began building eight new tunnels at a deeper level in 1940. These were to act as more secure public shelters while the war continued, but there were long-term plans to use them as the basis for new express tube lines. In fact, the tunnels were used exclusively for military purposes from their completion in 1942 until the flying bomb attacks in 1944 when five were opened up as civilian shelters. The express tube idea was never implemented.

London Transport not only transported and sheltered both civilians and military personnel; it also made an important contribution to the war effort through its workshops. The London Aircraft Production group was set up in 1941 in association with four motor companies – Chrysler, Duple, Express Motor and Body Works and Park Royal Coach Works – to build Halifax heavy bombers. More than 700 were manufactured over a four-year period by a workforce of whom 80 per cent had no previous engineering experience. Over half of them were women. London Transport's building department made parts for trestle bridges, landing craft, pontoon floats and aircraft turntables. The engineering shops at Charlton tram and trolleybus overhaul works were turned over to the manufacture of ammunition and gun parts, while the bus and coach department built nearly a thousand lorries, overhauled War Department vehicles and made parts for tanks. At Acton railway works, London Transport overhauled landing craft motors and carried out repair work on tanks, converting many for operation in water up to ten feet deep. This work reached a peak in the months leading up to the Allied invasion of Europe in June 1944. As 'D' Day approached, London Transport buses conveyed six infantry divisions to their ships and assault craft at the Channel ports. Over the next few weeks many of them were required again to transfer returning army casualties from trains to hospitals.

By this time London was under attack from a sinister new weapon, the 'V1' flying bomb. The heaviest 'V1' assaults were between June and August 1944, but from 8th September the Germans began using the more powerful 'V2' rocket bombs as well and continued to hit London until the end of March 1945. Damage was much less serious than during the Blitz of 1940–41, but the final months of bombing prompted another wave of evacuation and contributed to a new reduction in London Transport's passenger carrying levels, which had increased again in 1942–43 with greater mobilisation for war work and the arrival of US Forces in London. Quite apart from the enormous problems involved in trying to maintain services with badly damaged vehicles and property, London Transport was finding itself unable to cover its costs in 1944–45. By the end of the war, fares had gone up by 10 per cent, but costs had soared by 45 per cent.

The war in Europe ended on 8th May 1945, 'VE' Day. Six years of conflict had taken a considerable toll on London Transport. Six hundred and ninety-nine members of staff were killed on active service in HM Forces. In the air attacks on London, 426 staff were killed and nearly 3,000 injured. Two hundred and forty-one road vehicles and 19 railway cars were totally destroyed by enemy action and many others badly damaged. A vast amount of repair work to London Transport's bombed or neglected property was also necessary. Reconstruction began almost immediately, but a period of post-war austerity lay ahead.

(Parts of this introduction appeared previously in *The London Transport Golden Jubilee Book*)

Oliver Green

1 'A Time for Preparation, Effort and Resolve'

LONDON without its rumbling red omnibuses, its clanging trams, its rushing Underground trains, its gliding trolleybuses, its streamlined coaches and its moving staircases—such a London would be almost uninhabitable.

And who could assess this better than Hitler? So it was that the vast network of communications which had been built up in peacetime by the London Passenger Transport Board over 2,000 square miles within a radius of twenty-five miles from the centre of the capital, became a priority target for the Luftwaffe, when bombing began in the summer of 1940. By VE-day 181 members of the staff of London Transport had been killed on duty, with another 1,867 more or less seriously injured, while buses, trams, trolleybuses and railways cars had received damage on nearly nine thousand occasions as a result of blast, incendiaries, bombs, V.1's and V.2's. Some were damaged on four and even five different occasions.

But—'*the services must run. If they don't, London stops*'. That was the instinctive feeling of all the men and women of the Board, and it was only their unflinching determination that made it possible for the public to obey the famous exhortation '*Carry on, London*'.

Actually, the story behind their resolve goes back to Munich, and even to early 1937, when the Board appointed an A.R.P. Committee and, shortly afterwards, issued a manual of instructions to all members of the staff, many of whom were formed into 24-hour squads, specially equipped with protective clothing. Work on the organisation of air-raid precaution measures began at various depots. Members of the staff attended a series of lectures and demonstrations, two thousand of them qualifying as sub-instructors. After passing an examination they gave talks to the staff and formed squads for rescue and demolition in addition to first aid, fire fighting and decontamination. To maintain a high standard, monthly exercises in all squad duties were arranged.

Meanwhile, too, progressive arrangements were made for the reduction of the mileage of the omnibus and coach fleet, the blackout of premises and vehicles, the de-centralisation of stores and records, and investigation into the use of alternative fuels, and the staff position arising both from conscription and from the absorption of women employees. In 1914 there was no control by the Ministry as compared with 1939, when labour was handled by the Ministry from the very outset in such a way that employers knew at a given moment exactly how many of their staff were likely to be called up.

With regard to the Schedule of Reserved Occupations whereby drivers were reserved, it became evident that as the war, when it came, would almost certainly be mechanised, the availability of suitable bus drivers would soon become exhausted. It was therefore decided to train bus conductors as drivers to act as reserves in case of necessity. The risk of the call-up of bus conductors (who were not reserved) was not particularly serious, as experience of the ability of women to do this work had been obtained in World War I.

Whatever his political enemies may have said in the past about the late Neville Chamberlain's appeasement policy, the evidence of the Nuremberg trials reveals that the respite bought by him at Munich in 1938 was most unpopular with Hitler, who realised that invaluable time would be given for

Exercises were arranged. . . . Of the staff who did not leave on War Service, nearly one half was trained in some form of A.R.P. work within London Transport.

Great Britain to prepare herself, at least partially, for the inevitable contest. The London Passenger Transport Board was no exception to the rest of the great organisations which profited by the interlude.

Unlike the others, however, it had only been in existence for five years and had already embarked on a vast programme of improvement and new works which included a £40,000,000 five-year development scheme in conjunction with the Main Line Railways and with the support of the Government. By the early part of 1938, £23,000,000 worth of work had already been completed. More than half the entire fleet of buses and coaches had been replaced by modern and more efficient vehicles. The question was to what extent the remainder of the programme was to be carried out, in spite of the sudden threat of war. Generally speaking, the railway extensions were continued, and the new trolleybus programme maintained, though engineering departments previously engaged on new works schemes were switched to special war duties.

The very first purchases to be used in the event of war were sand, sandbags and shovels. But buying did not cease there. In the order book there appear, consecutively, purchases of hot-water bottles, blackout materials, bleach ointment, lamp shades, milk jugs, dustbins, sand containers, tourniquets, yellow soap, spare canvases for stretchers, fire-

Clippies of 1916. It was assumed (and rightly) that their daughters, if these were required, would be as good, if not better.

extinguishers, sal volatile and Primus stoves. In addition to these finished articles, the purchasing department bought vast quantities of raw materials, as well as arranging for five special dumps of girders, heavy timbers, rails and sleepers, and other materials for possible war damage purposes, and two substantial dumps of coal for emergencies.

Nobody could possibly foretell at that time what form the war would take. The London hospitals had been officially informed that three air raids, each causing 8,000 casualties, could be confidently expected on the opening day of hostilities. Poison gas was naturally presumed. Thousands of pounds had therefore to be spent not only on protective clothing, but on everything which went with it, such as clothes hangers for its efficient storing, larynx-microphones for the use of telephone operators, handbells to announce the gas *All Clear*, paper labels lettered 'DANGER—GAS' and all those wooden, sulphur-coloured structures which would have turned red in the event of poison gas. The menace of ordinary bombs called for untold quantities

of fire-extinguishers, fire-pumps, static-water tanks, stirrup pumps and—when the supply of the latter had been exhausted—garden-syringes! Even periscopes were bought for installation at various control points so that key men could observe the damage in the immediate neighbourhood in safety.

At one moment the buying programme was so hectically comprehensive that a senior official in the purchasing department announced that there was only one item which had been overlooked. He was asked with anxiety what could possibly have been forgotten. He replied, 'A truss of straw. We're all going barmy.' After events proved that this 'mad' buying was fully justified. The portable lavatories and refuse-ejectors alone were worth their weight in gold when the shelterers invaded the Underground system in their thousands.

But do you remember the Redhill containers? They consisted of a scoop and a bucket, the idea being that the householder, when confronted with an incendiary, approached it warily, before popping it safely into his bucket. . . . Even more optimistic was the purchase of garden rakes when no more scoops were available. History happily does not relate what would have happened when explosive incendiaries appeared on the scene, and the bucket blew up.

Surprising as it may appear to the layman, however, the executives of the Board were by no means so concerned with the menace of bombing and its attendant fires and possible poison gas, as with the danger from water. Old Father Thames, almost the Patron Saint of Cockneys, Old Father Thames who enabled London to develop into the world's greatest seaport, became overnight a terrifying ogre. The Board's railway system was immediately vulnerable to flooding if any of the under-river tunnels were holed or if the Victoria Embankment were breached, or if water mains and sewers were damaged and discharged directly into the tunnels, station entrances and escalator chambers.

The under-river tunnels consisted of two Bakerloo Line tunnels between Charing Cross and Waterloo, two Northern Line tunnels between the same stations, two Northern Line tunnels between Bank and London Bridge, two East London Line tunnels between Wapping and Rotherhithe, two disused tunnels between Monument and London Bridge and one disused tunnel (the old Hampstead Line terminus) which ran partly under the river at Charing Cross. A single bomb dropped in the proximity of the Charing Cross–Waterloo tunnels could have swamped half London's Underground System, flooding from Shepherds Bush to Liverpool Street, from Hammersmith to Kings Cross, from Clapham Common to Euston, and from Elephant & Castle to Marylebone. The only safe sections, in fact, would have been those between Marylebone and Queens Park, Euston and Highgate, Euston and Hampstead, Kings Cross and Southgate, Clapham Common and Morden, Moorgate and Finsbury Park. Even in these areas there were sewers and water mains near the stations which, if breached, could have caused amazing damage locally.

It was a matter of discussion between the experts as to what the exact results would be if one of the Thames tunnels were holed by enemy action. It might be that the trains would act as a stopper and dam the water, or that the water pressure would carry the train along with the flood. It was also possible that the silt from the river bed would quickly clog the breach. But the actual effect was, of course, dependent on the size and position of the hole and the state of the tide at the time.

One thing was certain. A direct hit on any of the Thames tunnels in their unprotected state would have meant at least a year's hard work before the train service could be put in full running order again.

The first thing to do, therefore, was to build flood-gates and have diaphragms to erect as a second line of defence, at every vulnerable point. Nobody knew how much grace would be given by Hitler. Nor had the building of flood-gates any engineering precedent, the limited space in which they would have to operate presenting a technical problem of the greatest magnitude.

The obvious solution would have been to construct swinging lock-gate type doors, but there was no room for them. Another headache was the necessity of carrying an electric track through an opening which had to be sealed against a heavy pressure of water when the gates were closed. The platforms at Charing Cross were also isolated by means of electrically-operated sector flood-gates at the passage openings. Fully signalled crossovers were installed for turning back the trains when the flood-gates were closed.

Ultimately twenty-five flood-gates were constructed at a cost of a quarter of a million pounds. Another three-quarters of a million had to be spent on constructing various protective devices in the neighbourhood of important water mains and sewers, and many thousands of pounds on the installation of secondary safety devices for rapid erection in the event of damage to the flood-gates.

In the meantime the Munich crisis made it necessary for precautions to be taken, then and there, against war, and from September 27 to October 7, 1938, the under-river tunnels between Charing Cross and Waterloo, both

Flood-gates—an expensive precaution. But without their assurance the Underground would have been at a standstill during all 'Alerts'.

Bakerloo and Northern Line, were blocked with concrete. During this emergency period the Bakerloo service was reversed from south to north at Piccadilly Circus, and the Northern service from south to north at Strand. It took twenty-four hours to insert these concrete blocks and four days to remove them. Concrete blocks were also inserted in all cross-passages on the Bakerloo Line and Northern Line where they crossed beneath the Thames.

Flood-gates were planned for the south end of the under-river portion of the East London Line. These flood-gates were of the vertical lift type and could be closed by gravity. Flood-gates to protect the system in the event of the Victoria Embankment being breached were erected on the District Line at Charing Cross and as far west as South Kensington.

Another tricky job was to install hydrophones in the river bed at suitable points so that the impact of a delayed-action bomb or mine falling near any of the under-river tunnels could be promptly detected. The sound was recorded electrically in the control room at the South Kensington headquarters of the Chief Engineer. Another device showed at any given moment of the day or night, the exact height of the Thames and whether the tide was rising or falling, so that when water-level conditions were favourable the District Line gates need not be closed in *Alerts*.

The flood-gates, which could be worked by hand if their electric drive failed (two alternative sources of electric supply were provided), were manned day and night and the time required to close them was half a minute.

The key to the collective control of all the flood-gates was a small room with bronze doors in the passage between the Piccadilly and Northern Lines at Leicester Square.

Speed and determination. Fire-fighting squads were formed from the staff, equipped and trained to high efficiency. Much of this training was done in spare time.

(Above) *A second-line defence against the river—diaphragms.* (Below) *Spades were trumps—ballast goes to make the Underground safe.*

Thousands of people must have passed it every day without realising the immense importance of what occurred behind the back of the sturdy police constable, sole safeguard against sabotage.

It is an unpretentious little room, about twelve feet wide and twenty feet long, equipped with three swivel-chairs, six telephones, a big switchboard and the actual control mechanism. This looks rather like an iron upright-grand piano except that it is only half the width. Above it is a wooden contraption with the electrical impulses which indicate the level of the tides. There are coloured lights alongside each of the numerals representing the flood-gates. Here sat the controller who, by pulling a 3-inch lever, could guarantee that every flood-gate attendant would be warned of an impending bomb, doodle-bug or rocket. The turning of the lever gave the signal for the immediate closing of the flood-gates.

But it must not be thought that, when the engineering problems of gate installation were successfully overcome, the rest was simple. The Signal Engineer's department had to provide measures ensuring the safe operation of the gates, and as will be seen, this was an involved problem. It had to be ensured that the signals given by the Controller were properly transmitted and acknowledged, these being the *Warnings*, *Alerts* and *All Clears*. The Controller had to know at any time whether individual gates were actually open or closed. The foregoing equipment covered the flooding risks, but with doors passing across the tracks, train safety was at least as important. It was also highly desirable to avoid shutting passenger trains in the under-river tunnels.

Diaphragms were provided at the gate sites to permit opportunity being given for trains to emerge before the gates were closed. To reduce the possibility of waiting for this, arrangements had to be made to stop trains safely before entering a tunnel immediately after the *Alert*. To prevent gates moving into the path of oncoming trains gate-locking and interlock signals were needed, as well as other arrangements to avoid the risk of trains running into gates already shut.

Many other safeguards had to be devised. Arrangements were made with the Government for priority telephone messages to be sent to specified offices and properties of the Board in the event of air raids. All properties were surveyed and a programme drawn up to make them safe for passengers and staff. Buildings and structures had to be strengthened. Glass had to be removed from roofs and replaced with sheeting, or protection provided by close-mesh wire.

On September 23, 1938, arrangements were made for the construction of trench shelters, first-aid and control points, shelters at Chiswick and Acton among other places, and for the adaptation of pits at garages as shelters for the staff. On September 27, 1938, the Munich crisis had become so acute that 1,500 men at a time were drawn from the Chiswick and Acton works to dig trenches and, in conjunction with a mechanical excavator, provided in four days trench shelters for 2,700 people.

Instructions were also given for the erection of a new fire-station at Chiswick, and a well was sunk which gave a capacity of 400 gallons per hour for five hours' continuous fire-fighting.

Other protective measures such as blackout were pushed ahead so that the Chief Engineer (Buses and Coaches) was able to state that all essential precautionary measures would have been available for operation on October 1, 1938, if a state of war had been declared.

As early as July, 1938, the Board had been approached by the Home Office with a view to planning the conversion of three hundred Green Line coaches into ambulances at twenty-four hours' notice. Designs were prepared and a set of equipment having been found satisfactory, the Chief Engineer (Buses and Coaches) received instructions on September 5, 1938, to get ready. Within a fortnight the whole of this equipment had been

distributed to the garages and on September 19 several sample coaches were converted at various garages. (Two days before war was declared every Green Line coach was withdrawn and over 400 of the fleet were converted into ambulances within five hours and most were transferred immediately from their country garages to the London area, where they came under the orders of the Ministry of Health.)

Two eventualities were considered possible: (a) the development of an unexpected emergency at practically no notice, and (b) declaration of war after a reasonable period of warning.

As far as surface vehicles were concerned, the emergency plan provided for a carton containing appropriate paper discs and a tube of glue in every vehicle to obscure various lights and headlamps. The second plan provided for the storing of more permanent equipment which consisted of a metal headlamp mask with a horizontal slot aperture, and cowls to fit on the electric light bulbs inside the vehicles. It also involved the removal of bulbs from fog-lamps, offside headlamps, side lights, destination and route number boxes, and platform lights. The headlamp masks were manufactured in accordance with Home Office instructions at the end of 1938. Later on the Home Office changed its mind. Ultimately .006 ft. candles was intimated as the legal maximum, this

amounting to the amount of light provided by the striking of a match, and making it almost impossible for the conductors to distinguish between silver and copper, quite apart from punching tickets correctly; while the drivers could scarcely see beyond the end of their nose.

Windows had to be protected with fabric. Plans had to be made to fit signal-boxes with steel shutters and to re-arrange station ventilation fans to deter the entry of poison gas. The blackout of stations, depots and offices, compliance with lighting restrictions and the importance of affording protection against blast, presented a major problem because of the conflicting demand for the need to maintain normal travel services.

Protection against blast was originally provided by sandbags, later by the erection of blast walls and the bricking-up of windows. Other protective measures included the closing of certain station entrances, strengthening of buildings and the provision of steel shelters for use in exposed positions. Glass screens had to be removed from ticket halls and trains, and anti-splinter netting affixed to booking offices, signal cabins and train windows. Emergency breakdown equipment was provided at thirty different points, together with gangs of specially trained men, who knew exactly what to do in the event of a bombing or gas attack. A scheme was prepared whereby they could notify the proper authorities as soon as the incident occurred. Each man was allocated a war station, the original plan involving three shifts in every twenty-four hours. (Later, so much damage was done and the staff was so depleted that two twelve-hour shifts had to be introduced.)

First-aid rooms were constructed at railway depots and works and at some of the garages. The road and railway staff was provided with steel helmets. Tanks and pits were kept filled in case the normal water supply failed. Key plants were dispersed. Telephone exchanges were duplicated. Emergency exchanges and control points were constructed

beyond the reach of bombs and gas. Emergency repair squads were held in readiness. Hooters had to be provided to give staff warnings at offices and depots. Railway traffic controls were duplicated at existing points and a special control for road service was set up underground at Oval Station.

In April, 1939, schemes for the evacuation of certain classes of the civilian population were finalised and the preparations of the necessary schedules begun. The people affected were schoolchildren, mothers with children under the age of five, handicapped children, expectant mothers, old persons, blind persons, mental cases and hospital staff. The scheme for the first two categories provided for their conveyance from assembly points, usually schools, to a railway station. It was planned that the other categories were to be conveyed direct by road to the reception areas, some of them a considerable distance away.

Undeterred by wishful-thinking newspaper headlines which announced that there was no possibility of war, the Board continued its active preparations to cope, as far as was possible, with any emergency which might arise. Everything was in such apple-pie order that when, on August 24/25, 1939, the whole of the First, Second and Fifth Anti-Aircraft Divisions had to be moved immediately to their war stations in various parts of the Home Counties, the movement was completed without a hitch by the 489 omnibuses required. So too was the movement of Territorial Battalions of the Royal West Kents, the London Irish Rifles, the Middlesex, the East Surreys, the Essex and the Queen's Westminsters from their drill halls to different barracks in Greater London.

In the meantime, too, the intricate and

costly construction of the flood-gates and diaphragms was proceeding apace. On August 27, the Bakerloo Line was closed south of Piccadilly Circus for one day to aid the installation of the flood-gates. War stores were being amassed and every ounce of energy which could be diverted from normal peace-time activities was concentrated on preparations for the Day.

2 First Effects: the Blackout and the Evacuation

THE WAR'S first rude, dramatic effect upon the public was the imposition of the blackout on September 1, 1939. From that day onwards every omnibus was compelled to run with reduced lighting, which naturally led to a general slowing down of traffic. Headlights and the interior lights of omnibuses and coaches were covered with the cowls already described, the slits of which were so small that drivers could scarcely see a yard in front of them as they attempted to negotiate the darkened streets. (Much later, as a result of the bombing of Paris, and after a number of tests with a dozen different protective devices, it was decided that netting was the best protection for windows of all rolling-stock against blast.)

On the same day, September 1, the Railway Executive Committee came into being. This was the agency whereby the Ministry of Transport was able to give instructions under the Railway Control Order, 1939. In fact, it had existed in skeleton fashion for nearly a year. Now it suddenly came to life. The principle was that the ordinary management of railway undertakings was to remain in the hands of existing railway staffs, the functions of the Railway Executive Committee being to ensure that the railways and the London

Passenger Transport Board made the greatest possible contribution to the war effort.

The same red-letter day saw the start of the evacuation from London. In four days more than half a million people, largely children, were conveyed out of the danger zone by the Board's vehicles. This involved journeys of considerable distances, some of which made it necessary for the omnibuses to be two days on the road. Many drivers had no sleep for 36 hours. Double-deck and single-deck vehicles were used. Expectant mothers were sent as far afield as Oxford, Cambridge, Northampton, Bury St. Edmunds, Eastbourne and Trowbridge. A high percentage of blind persons were sent to Luton. Crippled children were taken to such places as Littlehampton, Lowestoft and Weston-super-Mare. The mental cases were dispersed among the various mental institutions in London to prevent an undue number being housed in one building.

The popularity of holiday camps, which had reached such high proportions between the two wars, made the reception of the evacuees much easier than would otherwise have been possible. But it says a great deal for the enterprise and resourcefulness of the drivers and conductors employed on this vast humanitarian scheme, that not a single injury was reported, nor a single meal missed. Great care had previously been taken by the Board to ensure that the double-deck omnibuses, driven by men who in many cases had never been outside London, did not meet with any

mishap. Special itineraries to enable the double-deckers to avoid low bridges were arranged. Some of these involved considerable detours. There were instances of Reception Committees not being ready for the evacuees. When this regrettably occurred, the drivers took it upon themselves to billet their passengers arbitrarily at the most convenient spot.

But of all the Board's services, the Underground railways carried the major load of evacuees. Parties were entrained at seventy-two Underground stations in the central area and carried to outlying stations from which they completed their journeys to reception areas, either by Main Line Railway trains or by London Transport's own omnibuses. At Ealing Broadway Station alone—believe it or not—101,000 persons were passed through.

Hospital patients were removed by Green Line coaches, converted so swiftly into ambulances built to carry eight to ten stretcher cases each. Patients in Bart's were taken direct to King Edward VII hospital at Windsor. Patients in Guy's, St. Thomas's, King's College, St. James's and St. Giles's Hospitals were taken to Clapham Junction,

where they were transferred to the Southern Railway. Addison Road, as it was then called, became the rail head for patients in eighteen other hospitals, including St. Mary's, St. George's, the Royal Free, Charing Cross, 'U.C.H.' and the London.

A perusal of the details of this astonishing evacuation shows a series of bewildering statistics. Suffice it to say that the trams and trolleybuses also did yeoman service. Nearly thirteen thousand evacuees were taken to Waterloo alone. Nor was the catering side overlooked. Emergency refreshment services were arranged at various stations.

All these thousands of persons, some of them small children . . . and not one mishap of any kind. That is the astonishing and supremely creditable feat which stands out in the record of this colossal mass movement carried out, of course, in conjunction with the Main Line Railways and the L.C.C.

Its success would, however, have been impossible but for the co-operation of the public, which in turn would have been impossible without instructions supplied by the Board. Thousands and thousands of posters, instructions, slips and direction signs had to

GOOD BYE — HITLER

be printed, issued and fixed so the evacuation could proceed smoothly. As certain stations were reserved for the despatch of children, many notices had to be printed to explain the procedure for evacuees and to warn other members of the public that their travel facilities would be curtailed during certain periods of the day.

The question of traffic direction, tickets to purchase, carriage for luggage, lists of stations affected, working of special non-stop trains also had to be made public. In addition to the evacuation of children, there were members of the civil population who were being evacuated and for whom special arrangements were made to cover all eventualities, and for whom printed instructions had to be prepared. It must be remembered that there were thousands of Servicemen to be transported across London, for whom traffic direction had to be clear. The public had to be told of alternative means of travel and movement in lieu of the limits placed on their normal mode of travel. Special road services were run to provide alternative travel and this necessitated notices on buses, trams and trolleybuses, of the points between which the service operated, the availability of tickets, and where to pick up the special services. At this time the engineering departments were working on strengthening station walls and

on erecting bulkheads, which in many cases caused the complete closing of sections of the line and for which special direction for alternative travel had to be provided. The work of the Publicity Department was connected with all phases of the operation of the road and rail services and it had to be cognisant of all that was happening so that the travelling public could be told accurately what they had to do to travel between certain points; when to travel, how, why; and certainly to make the alternative directions foolproof and reasonable.

As the sections of line were made ready for wartime operations, the traffic directions reverted to almost normal, and re-direction had to be dealt with. With a depleting staff, difficulties of travel, the Department carried on, and although the printing sections were busy, it must not be forgotten that all that was printed had to be displayed, and the actual posting section (the outdoor men), sign makers, sign fitters, bill posters, had a busy time in dealing with the display of the material that was printed. An all-night printing service was arranged so that urgent work could be obtained at any time of the day or night.

It became obvious that the Board's services, surface and below ground, were liable to curtailment or interruption at any time,

and arrangements were always at hand whereby emergency operation could be made available for all traffic direction, via posters, signs and slips, at very short notice. Stations were closed collectively and opened singly as they were available—all of which required special publicity and reprinting of existing notices. There were restrictions on the use of paper, withdrawal of travel facilities, and all were covered from every angle—Press, posters, signs, slips—the posting instructions were at times most complicated.

At 11.0 a.m. on September 2, 1939, senior engineers of the Board tore open envelopes containing sealed orders and proceeded to insert concrete plugs at every available point not yet protected by flood-gates, of which eight were already in operation at the strategic tunnels between Charing Cross and Waterloo. Soon after the declaration of war, every tunnel was safe. Nothing was left to chance. Even the old Strand–Charing Cross Loop tunnel was sealed at either end; it had been out of use for years. The fantastic sequel was that within three days of the bombing of London a year later, it received a direct hit, the only direct hit suffered by any of the Board's Thames tunnels. Dismay at this was coupled with satisfaction that the proper precautions had been taken. A section over two hundred yards long was flooded by the river which would otherwise have swamped the Underground network for miles in all directions. Even now, in 1947, the Thames is still in possession of that particular section of the tunnel. But we are going ahead too fast.

Early in 1939 complete lists of every man's commitments were prepared, and when war was declared a number of staff who were Territorials were on their annual training. Others being reservists had been called up for refresher courses. These men, naturally, did not return to work. In addition, all staff with obligations for Service were immediately instructed to report for duty and, within a few days, nearly two thousand five hundred drivers, conductors and officials had left their normal employment.

Why they disappeared! On September 1, 1939, all Green Line coaches were withdrawn; within five hours 400 had been converted into ambulances.

This at once caused great difficulty at the Board's garages and depots from which varying numbers of men of different grades left suddenly. The staffing of vehicles was further complicated by the necessity to place a number of single-deck omnibuses at the disposal of the London Fire Brigade to assist local fire brigades in provincial towns to deal with any conflagrations caused by enemy action. (Later on these omnibuses went to Coventry, Birmingham, Bristol, Southampton and Stockport. Drivers were told beforehand that they were likely to be away for several days and they would therefore be wise to take necessities with them, and arrangements had to be made for the refuelling of the vehicles *en route.*)

The Board also undertook to supply as many as a hundred omnibuses to the Police in case of emergency. A scheme was prepared showing the police stations to which the buses would report and the Board's garages from which the buses would be allocated. From the picking-up point onwards they were to operate under Police instructions. From time to time a number of them were used by the Police in this way, but fortunately the scheme as a whole did not have to operate.

In less than three weeks the supplies of

petrol and fuel oil were cut by 25 per cent. This made it necessary to withdraw a large number of vehicles on the central bus section too quickly for it to be possible to revise all the time and duty schedules. By January, 1940, 839 central buses were withdrawn from service entirely. Others were withdrawn during the normal hours between 10.0 a.m. and 4.0 p.m. and the majority were curtailed in the early evening owing to the blackout. The saving in mileage was about 30 per cent. Trams and trolleybuses were naturally not affected by the petrol restrictions and continued to operate their ordinary schedules except for certain curtailments owing to the blackout, made locally by the traffic officials.

As soon as possible a complete new set of timetables was prepared. Running times had to be revised to meet blackout conditions and also the reduction in traffic on the streets. Rotas were arranged to reduce the maximum time a man was required to drive in the blackout and, generally speaking, the service was reduced to a minimum except during the peak hours. So thorough was the overhaul and so successful its results, that peak-hour services were maintained practically in their entirety. In no instances were people whose sole means of travelling was the bus deprived of transport, and it was not until a year later that journeys after 10.30 p.m. from central London were discontinued. This was in spite of the fact that, at the request of the Army authorities, over five hundred of the best drivers were allowed to volunteer to train Army recruits.

As a means of providing more accommodation on the road services, the number of passengers permitted to stand on the lower deck was raised from five to eight, and later to twelve.

Fortunately for the railway department of the Board, there was a considerable reduction in the volume of traffic. This was chiefly due to the staggering effects of war upon business, the evacuation of offices and the imposition of the blackout. But it was also partly due to the loss of facilities caused by the closing of different railway stations for various reasons. Some were closed in order to facilitate protective works against flooding.

Four special suites of underground offices were fitted up in disused passages and platforms at Down Street, Dover Street, Hyde Park Corner, Knightsbridge and Holborn, accommodating about 350 people. Down Street was equipped for the Railway Executive Committee. Dover Street was arranged for the Chairman and the Board's principal officers. It was fitted as a complete suite for sleeping, feeding and working. These offices also had access from the Piccadilly Line at Green Park Station.

Another disused station became the headquarters of Anti-Aircraft Control. Part of the tunnel at Aldwych was commandeered by the Office of Works for the storage of valuables. Later the disused stations of South Kentish Town, British Museum and City Road became shelters too. Later on still, a part of Earls Court Station was used for the manufacture of torpedo sights and other war equipment.

Traffic during the late evening became increasingly light. Conforming with the drastic blackout regulations, all stations in the open and trains whilst travelling over open sections of the line were completely devoid of light after dark except for three tiny lamps in each car. But it was soon realised that some modification was essential for purposes of safety and in the public interest. This was finally secured after a number of conferences with the Minister of Home Security, the Minister of War Transport, and the various Service departments, with the result that special safety reading-lamps were manufactured and installed within 14 days.

The effect of the blackout on the trams was almost worse than it was on the railways. The frequency of the services and the density of street traffic made it necessary in peacetime to handle many major track maintenance jobs during the night. These included replacing worn tram rails and steel crossings, repairs by welding and cleaning of the conduit under the tracks. All these operations required a specially strong light.

An entirely new problem was presented by the blackout and the need to perform all this work in daylight with full car services running and ordinary street traffic at its maximum. Worse still, every job of filling-in or re-paving had to be finished on the day it began, to prevent danger to emergency service vehicles speeding through the unlit streets during the night. The situation looked almost hopeless on some routes where the time available for exchanging the new rails for the old was only a few minutes. And as the road had to be paved-in again before blackout time, each day's work involved breaking-out the

paving, clearing the old rail from its cement and bitumen setting, freeing it from its joints with the adjacent rails, anchors, tie-rods and other fastenings, lifting out the old rail, laying, gauging, packing and fastening the new rail, adjusting the slot, re-setting the paving and finally tidying up and clearing away tools, materials and rubbish so that the road would be completely clear before the working gang went home.

Renewal work at junctions could not be carried out without some occasional indulgence by the traffic operators. Fortunately this constituted only a small amount of the total track mileage and so, by choosing times during the week-end when tram services were lightest and by working short lengths of single line, essential work was accomplished without serious interference.

At certain points where the road was very

The 'ops room' of A.A. Command—the defence of London's sky controlled from underground, within a few feet of the passing trains.

much cramped and ordinary traffic excep-
tionally heavy, a special dispensation was obtained to permit of a little night work being
done. The lighting was arranged in such a
way that it could be extinguished immediately on receipt of an air-raid warning.

Electric arc welding creates such a brilliant
light and is such a lengthy process that it
seemed out of the question. The obvious solution of enclosing the welder and the job was
found impracticable because of the gases
emitted by the welding process. By careful
improvisation, however, the necessary screen-
ing was designed to cover just the work and
the workman's hands only, observation of the
work being made through a peep-hole.

The routine cleaning of the tramway conduit under wartime conditions presented
another major problem. But this, too, was
solved by the ingenuity of the Board's
engineers.

3 Dunkirk—and After: Women take up the Task

THE WINTER of 1939 passed slowly into
the early spring of 1940. This was
the phoney war period and every advantage was taken of the respite to build up
further stores, to finish the remaining flood-
gates and generally to complete the transition
from peace to war. By December, 1939, six
more flood-gates had been finished, and the
Northern Line resumed working between
Strand and Kennington, working between
Moorgate and London Bridge being resumed
in May, 1940.

Every day more war workers were coming
to London. This demanded more prompt and
more punctual travel than ever before,
although there were fewer vehicles and less
petrol. This was the problem facing the

Board, the body responsible for the conveyance of the greatest and most concentrated
and yet tremendously scattered congregation
of people in the world, to tasks more important and more urgent than the nation had
ever before demanded.

The first consideration was the movement
of munition workers whose travel movements
were concentrated at half-hourly intervals
from before dawn to 8.0 a.m. Half a million
of them were involved within a radius of
fifteen miles from the centre of the City. And
every one of them needed punctual service.
Individuals had to be at their factories and
workshops at exact moments between 6.0 a.m.
and 8.0 a.m. and taken home with almost
equal regularity between 4.30 p.m. and
7.0 p.m. Besides the munition workers there
were large numbers of other people employed
in different industries, not to mention shop
assistants and black-coat workers arriving at
their places of employment between 8.30 a.m.
and 10.0 a.m.

Expert observation at Underground stations in the central London area showed that
26,000 people would arrive in one fifteen-
minute period while during the preceding
quarter of an hour it was only 15,000. At
night on the homeward journeys, 35,000
persons demanded accommodation in one
period of fifteen minutes, double the number
of those travelling half an hour earlier. The
Board made every effort to persuade the
Government to grant statutory powers to
stagger working hours. One of the objections
raised was the difficulties which would be
caused by the necessary adjustment of over-
time. And what of Friday nights? There will
always be a rooted antipathy to the staggering
of pay days. Housewives—how could they
be tackled? Unfortunately for themselves,
they have no Trade Union and therefore no
official spokesman. All these problems were
confronting the Board during the early
months of the war.

Conditions on the Western Front were
practically static. The 51st Division had just
moved into position east of Metz. Casualties,

except for road accidents to despatch riders, were infinitesimal. Men were coming on leave, and special leave buses were inaugurated for their convenience.

Then came May 10, bringing in its wake thousands of hysterical, homeless refugees from Holland, Belgium and France. Double-deck omnibuses were made ready to pick up these war refugees at short notice as they arrived at the Main Line stations. Addison Road Station was used a great deal. From here the unfortunate foreigners were conveyed to rest centres at such places as Alexandra Palace and Wembley Stadium (which specialised in Gibraltarians). On one single day 812 buses were utilised for this purpose and many of them had to be given special hygienic treatment after such use.

The danger, soon realised, of the collapse of the French and Belgian armies now made it necessary to arrange a scheme to evacuate all the coastal towns in the areas of West Sussex, East Sussex and Kent, as well as Southend. Details were worked out so that all women and children could be evacuated in two days, and the remainder of the population within another three. The total number of the Board's buses needed for this job was 530 double-deckers and 20 single-deckers. Time schedules were prepared to cover the various moves: (1) from Main Line Railway stations or the Board's railway stations to reception areas, (2) between Main Line Railway stations, (3) from sleeping centres to meal centres and return, (4) distribution from sleeping centres to reception centres, (5) reception centres to billets.

Few of the people who lived in the thirty leading towns of West Sussex, East Sussex and Kent, headed by Bognor, Brighton, Hove, Worthing, Littlehampton, Hastings, Eastbourne, Margate, Ramsgate, Canterbury, Dover and Folkestone, could have known at the time that all possible plans for their safety had been made.

As a separate scheme, arrangements were made to supply ninety double-deckers to con-

Gun practice at Cleave Camp, Bude, in 1939. The 84th (London Transport) Heavy A.A. Regiment served in Norway, in Africa with the Eighth Army, and in Italy.

(Above) *Within eight weeks of its embodiment London Transport's Home Guard was inspected at Osterley.* (Below) *Members were detailed for the St. James's Palace Guard. Some 30,000 members of the staff served in London Transport's unit.*

vey refugees from the south-east coast areas.

Then came Anthony Eden's call-to-arms, and the L.D.V. was born overnight. As early as October, 1938, men of the Board had formed its own Territorial Unit; and the 84th (London Transport) Heavy A.A. Regiment, R.A., comprising Nos. 260, 261, 262, 263 Batteries, came into being. Now their comrades rallied to the call and six battalions were formed—two of busmen, two of tram and trolleybus men and two of railway and engineering staffs. The Commanding Officers were released by the Board for full-time service with the L.D.V. The Board also provided assistance in the way of clerical staff, accommodation and cars at the various battalion headquarters.

Within a matter of weeks a Unit parade of four thousand men was inspected by officers from London District. Only the Guard of Honour wore uniform, and that consisted merely of denim overalls. Soon it became evident that the battalions would have to be reorganised on a geographical basis with railwaymen, busmen, tram and trolleybus men being mixed in the same battalions wherever necessary. Later a seventh battalion was formed.

Most important was the special contingent of men detailed to patrol the Underground railway system. Apart from these special troops, the history of the seven battalions was that of all other Home Guard units. Arms and equipment, including Molotov cocktails, arrived in ever-increasing numbers and be-wildering variety. The Canadian Ross rifles were exchanged for P.17's. Thompson sub-machine carbines and Stens appeared. Northovers were superseded by Smith guns. Two-pounder anti-tank guns arrived and disappeared. The Spigot mortar became a favourite. All kinds of cock-eyed grenades came and went, only the good old 36 Mills grenade maintaining its reputation. In this connection it is pleasant to relate that the bombing instructors carried out their duties so well that there was not a single serious accident, much less loss of life.

Meanwhile the evacuation of Dunkirk took place and the coach ambulances were brought into use by the Government, additional numbers being transferred from the central area to garages in Kent and Surrey for use if required in connection with the evacuation. Emergency bus services were also operated between Coulsdon and Earlswood and Tonbridge and Guildford, the railway between these points being closed to normal traffic.

The evacuation of Dunkirk led in turn to another evacuation—of schoolchildren between June 13 and 18, 1940. During this period many thousands of children were conveyed to safety, for the probability of invasion had almost become a certainty.

Every preparation for the emergency was speeded up. Instructions were issued to the Board's staff on their duty in the event of the landing of enemy parachute troops. Drivers were warned to take all necessary steps to prevent vehicles from falling into enemy hands. A special wheel-locking device had already been fitted on all vehicles to immobilise them whenever they were left unattended. All garages were protected at night by armed guards. The staff were also instructed to make sure that their uniform did

. . . a bag of sand on every vehicle.

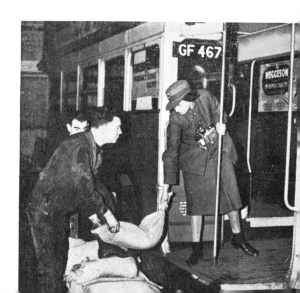

not fall into unauthorised hands, and to ignore all instructions other than those which appeared on the official notice boards. They had all been issued with civil defence respirators and steel helmets and a bag of sand was carried on every vehicle, with instructions for dealing with incendiaries.

Arrangements were made at all garages, within certain areas, for the immediate and complete immobilisation of petrol pumps in case of invasion. This also made it necessary for the removal of all signs indicating location of depots. As far as was practicable, maintenance work on road vehicles was transferred from night to day. There was, too, some relaxation in the peacetime standards of the appearance of vehicles, and whilst every effort was made to maintain the normal standard of interior cleanliness, it was not possible to do this on the outside.

On the engineering side, special safety-measures were taken to ensure that the services could be maintained in all circumstances. Some of the major repair work was dispersed to outlying garages. Vital machinery and stores were also dispersed and emergency stocks of essential materials were built up at strategic points. Administrative staff had already been dispersed. Emergency offices had been established in sports-ground pavilions or hastily-erected huts.

Further arrangements were made to guard the railway lines against sabotage and parachute attack. Volunteer patrols on foot watched the whole of the open sections of the railways throughout the twenty-four hours. These patrols continued throughout the 1940-41 period of heavy raids.

Dunkirk had another immediate effect. There were no longer enough men to go round, and the Board began to recruit women, as conductors, and, on the Underground railways, as booking clerks, porters and cleaners; and in the engineering grades. This substitution of women for men was at first confined to unskilled grades, but was later extended to semi-skilled and even skilled categories. Women usually started as labour-

ers and cleaners, but were given every encouragement to advance. Some actually became craftsmen.

The work the women did was very varied. They made the destination boards for buses, mounted and varnished the fare lists, stripped off old advertisements and posted new ones. At the garages they cleaned, washed, oiled and greased the vehicles, and in some instances helped to shunt the buses into position ready for the morning's run-out.

On the railways, women helped to maintain the permanent way and signals; they cleaned the cars; a night squad cleaned the tunnels; others cleaned and oiled the lift and escalator machinery, changed lamps, issued stores. They acted as porters and cleaners on the Underground.

At Country bus garages, women were employed as depot clerks, and as cleaners and greasers. Women staffed canteens at men's garages, and about fifteen hundred were kept busy preparing and serving meals for operating and engineering staff.

The Board's Electrical Department employed a small number of women at power stations, operating plant, cleaning boilers and general labouring.

These women had varied backgrounds, including, for example, waitresses and saleswomen, ballet dancers, mannequins, ships' stewardesses and receptionists. The age limits for employment were 21 and 36 years, and candidates were subject to a strict medical examination, a thorough training and probation, and a short period of supervised practical work. Welfare supervisors helped and guided them; canteens, rest-rooms and dormitories were provided for their comfort. Each was provided with a serviceable and becoming uniform.

As the supply of experienced men gradually decreased, it became evident that the task of maintaining rolling-stock could not be accomplished without upsetting the ordinary agreements between the management and the Trade Union representatives. So, many of these were temporarily waived so that men could be up-graded. Work in railway shops was particularly arduous, dirty and heavy. Women could not, therefore, be expected to compensate entirely for the loss of men whose workshop experience had been built up over many years. But generally the women proved efficient.

As the shortage of spare parts and materials grew more acute, there was a corresponding increase in the recovery of worn or damaged parts, while many materials in short supply had to be replaced by substitutes. Those which created the greatest need for substitutes were aluminium, rubber and paint. Sheet-steel or iron castings took the place of aluminium. Rubber was replaced by wood, steel and even by felt. Practically every enamel and varnish was replaced by synthetic, lower-grade substitutes, with a corresponding decrease in durability. Fortunately the reclamation of scrap was developed to a high level throughout the whole of the Board's organisation, and much time was devoted to the best way of obtaining further life from worn or broken parts.

Timber was salvaged and likely rags were collected. Worn rubber bulbs for omnibus-

drivers' hooters were replaced by a contrivance fashioned from leather and string. Wooden slatted seats saved moquette and rubber for which leather and other materials were also substituted.

Over six hundred tons of ticket pulp were saved in a single year. This was done by reducing the size and thickness of all road-transport tickets. The thickness was reduced from .012 to .008 inches, while the size of ninety per cent of the tickets, some of which were over $3\frac{1}{2}$ inches long, was reduced to a standard length of $2\frac{1}{4}$ inches. In addition seven hundred tons of paper pulp were salvaged from wasted tickets and obsolete tickets among other items.

Conductors were ordered to be as economical as possible in the use of auxiliary way-bills and copper bags. They were even asked to salvage the wire from their ticket packets and to be especially careful in operating their ticket punches and in urging passengers to put their tickets in the boxes provided.

Used oil was refined and used again and again. Waste wood and sawdust were employed for the development of producer gas at Chiswick works. A fleet of buses converted to run on producer gas saved $3\frac{1}{2}$ million gallons of petrol in a single year. Special service stations had to be arranged to handle the anthracite necessary to generate the gas. Each omnibus consumed about a ton of anthracite a week and required re-fuelling every eighty miles.

Lectures were given to garage staffs and methods of driving were specifically designed to keep down wear and tear. Drivers were also told to regulate the speed of their vehicles over any section of road which happened to be the worse for wear, to prevent damage to their buses.

Rubber handgrips were replaced by plastic knobs. Canvas hose was turned into mud flaps. Bus stops were reduced in number and nearly seven hundred buses were parked at certain points in central London, such as Hyde Park, Regent's Park and the Victoria Embankment, instead of running back empty or half empty to the garage—thus saving over

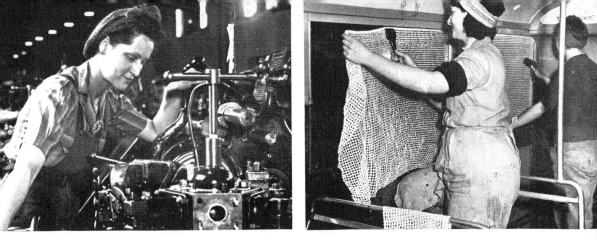

Women undertook all kinds of work—with enthusiasm and increasing efficiency. By the end of the war roundly 16,500 were employed on jobs formerly undertaken by men. Twenty women welfare supervisors were appointed: 75 rest rooms and 123 changing rooms were provided.

two million miles a year. Horsehair from obsolete railway carriage blinds was converted into brushes. All out-of-date files were sent for pulp. Bakelised cambric was used in various unexpected ways.

4 *The Battle of London begins*

T HE FIRST enemy bomb which caused casualties among the Board's personnel fell on Croydon aerodrome on August 15, 1940. At the earnest request of the Minister

of Aircraft Production, the Board had loaned two hundred fitters, electricians, bodymakers and assistant craftsmen to repair and service the pitifully few Hurricanes and Spitfires with which the Few won the Battle of Britain. They had been allocated mainly to the R.A.F. station at Henlow but also to the works of several manufacturers, one of which was at Croydon. (In addition to these a number of skilled men and members of the administrative staff of the Board had been loaned to the Ministry of Aircraft Production to plan aircraft factories, which they did with great success.)

The first enemy bomb which had a direct effect on the Board's actual services fell on August 16, 1940, at New Malden. This incident immediately showed the vulnerability of trolleybus wires and feeders to enemy action. These particular wires were repaired within $4\frac{1}{2}$ hours, but the local service was interrupted for nearly twenty-four hours by

Women 'fluffers' cleaning the track near Euston.

an unexploded bomb. To cope with the situation, the early morning shift were conveyed by lorry to the depot from which the trolley-buses were due to start their day's work. (There were occasions later on when no less than three tons of trolley wire had to be replaced in a matter of hours.)

South Wimbledon Substation of the Northern Line was also damaged by a bomb that afternoon. It was put temporarily out of commission, and two members of the staff were wounded, but in spite of considerable damage the repairs were achieved so quickly and efficiently that the train service between Tooting and Morden was suspended for only two hours.

Enemy air raids on the capital now became the order of the day, and the 'trickle' movement of evacuees from London became quite a flood. Fortunately the repair services were all ready for the blitz, with specially-equipped master breakdown lorries. The breakdown squads drove out with their lorries to give every means of assistance from service repairs during air raids to the lifting of D.A. bombs and land mines. They lifted vehicles, not necessarily the Board's, out of bomb craters. They hauled debris to aid A.R.P. and N.F.S. personnel in getting access to trapped victims. Hundreds of service vehicles, buses and trolleybuses, were towed away after having been either partially or wholly disabled. Vehicles of both types had frequently to be righted before the journey could begin. In almost every instance the services of these men and vehicles were required during active operations by the enemy and, in addition to the natural human fear of a heavy raid, there were the difficulties of the black-out, diversions over unknown roads, craters, debris and by-roads roped off because of the presence of unexploded bombs.

Daily air raids on the outskirts of London caused much damage and numbers of diversions. Most of the damage to buses was caused by bomb splinters, but one was damaged by machine-gun fire at Chaldon Cross Roads on August 18. Unexploded anti-aircraft shells were, too, a regular nuisance. There were no air raids on August 19 in the Greater London area, but six different omnibus routes had to be diverted on both Central and Country bus routes. Delayed action bombs in the Caterham district continued to cause diversions or curtailment of services locally. Bombs were dropped again on August 23 involving a number of diversions in the neighbourhood of Harrow Weald, and a shuttle bus service had to be operated between Sunningdale and Virginia Water on behalf of the Southern Railway.

Next day a bomb between Romford and Upminster necessitated the same arrangements being made on behalf of the L.M.S. Railway.

Every day the Luftwaffe was coming closer to central London, but Goering still held his hand as far as night bombing was concerned. Midnight *Alerts* were frequent, but the first heavy night raid took place on August 24.

In the meantime the delayed-action bombs and high explosives dropped in daylight gave the repair gangs and executives valuable experience, as well as a foretaste of what was to come. During this phase an anti-aircraft shell burst in Northfleet Garage, causing damage to fifteen of the Board's vehicles, not to mention the garage itself. Fortunately nobody was killed.

Continuous air-raid warnings caused dislocation of traffic, and by now the closing of the flood-gates was becoming a regular procedure. A melancholy entry in the Board's special air-raid report for September 4 shows that, owing to bombs being dropped on Vickers works, the special journeys for the staff were not required.

Another unexploded anti-aircraft shell damaged a gas main at Sidcup and caused a number of bus routes to be diverted. Further assistance had to be given to the Southern Railway in transporting passengers unable to travel because of D.A. bombs. More unexploded bombs in the vicinity of the Elephant & Castle caused the whole of this area to be banned to buses. Newington Causeway,

Newington Butts, New Kent Road, London Road and Walworth Road were all put 'out of bounds' by the Police.

On September 6, 1940, a bus left Croydon Garage at 5.30 p.m. in the direction of Liverpool Street. It was crowded. As it passed over London Bridge the Docks were one blazing mass of fire. As it passed Kennington on its return journey, the siren sounded again, but it had proceeded as far as Gresham Road, Brixton, when the driver heard a bomb descending in the neighbourhood of Camberwell. There were sixty-three people on board when he heard another bomb descending. He braked hard and pulled up. The bomb dropped in Barrow Road. If the driver had halted at his normal stop, his bus would have taken the full blast.

As it was, the vehicle was badly damaged. Great holes appeared instantaneously in the roof. But the passengers only suffered slight shock and cuts from glass splinters; every window in the vehicle being broken. The driver and conductor decided to direct the passengers into the neighbouring shelter and succeeded in doing so. There was only one casualty—an 18-year-old girl running with such panic-stricken speed towards the shelter that she hit the iron railings and knocked herself out.

The driver offered to continue as soon as it was safe, but did not reach Croydon Garage before 6.20 a.m. He went home and started work again at 8.0 a.m.

During this phase, buses, trams and trolley-buses were returning to their depots over four hours late, for the Police and A.R.P. wardens had instructions to stop all civilian traffic. The staff too, like everyone else, were at first inclined to take cover when they heard the sirens go, but afterwards they only did so when gunfire occurred in their immediate neighbourhood. Even this resulted in considerable loss of working-hours in offices and factories, and it was not long before the men only ceased to carry on when local bombing became intense.

Now came September 7. On that lovely Saturday afternoon 375 bombers and fighters came over in waves to bomb Woolwich Arsenal, Beckton Gas Works, South London, the Docks, the City, Westminster and, for no apparent reason, a crescent in Kensington. By six o'clock they had gone. But two hours eight minutes later the night bombers appeared and maintained their unimpeded attack until 4.30 a.m.

In the early days of the war the authorities had issued a fiat that the Tubes were not to be used as public air-raid shelters. Notices to this effect were posted all over the Underground stations in December, 1939, but the authorities did not know their Londoners, of whom thousands had used the Underground stations as air-raid shelters in the last war.

It has been said that one of the chief reasons for the continued greatness of Great Britain has been that the public always shows common sense in an emergency, whether political or warlike. It was sheer common sense on the part of the public to seek protection when the German bombers droned overhead on that night of September 7, 1940. And what protection could be better than that obviously provided by the Tubes? They therefore did the sensible thing and proceeded to utilise the safety and security provided underground.

They arrived in droves with their children and blankets, paid the 1½d. for tickets which gave them access to the Tube platforms. Those who found that the first station they selected was too crowded, moved over to the next. Some arrived with bulging shopping baskets, old coats, parcels of food, bottles of milk and ginger pop, and suitcases on which they squatted. One old woman proudly announced that she had brought enough cheese and tea-cakes for a fortnight, and indeed it was noted that she did not leave the East End railway platform which she had chosen for fourteen days, except to get a ten-minutes breath of fresh air when there was no air raid in progress.

The disused Tube station at Southwark was invaded by crowds who came in motor cars and even motor coaches, with cooking apparatus, vacuum-flasks and food. Some had come from as far away as Finchley and Forest Gate. The disused Tube of the Borough filled up rapidly, so much so that the residents of the Borough soon voiced an angry protest about strangers using *their* tunnel.

Curious scenes were observed on that first night and many others like it. Infants were publicly breast-fed. Bobby-sox girls titivated. Youngsters played cards. Old people snored in uneasy slumber on the hard, stone platforms. Fear, courage, sympathy, friendliness, resignation and cheerfulness were all displayed. Deck chairs and umbrellas, rugs, bed-time stories told by parents to their whimpering children, patient mothers knitting, girls in slacks, the smell of new cement and, shamefully enough, dozens of able-bodied youths who had jostled their way into the least uncomfortable positions—such was the scene. Then, when the last train had gone and the electric current had been cut off, they squatted along the track.

Reporters in their search to describe this new phenomenon gave them many nicknames in the newspapers. 'Squatters' and 'tunnellers' were the most popular.

As far as London Transport was concerned the situation clearly needed regulating. By 6.0 p.m. travellers found themselves unable to alight at various Tube stations without treading over already lolling bodies. By 8.0 p.m. few stations were passable, and by midnight aged people were being carried out into the fresh air and back again. At the very start, too, there were signs, quickly suppressed, of race hatred being fomented among the crowds of squatters.

Above ground the repair gangs worked coolly and methodically. Here is the story of one of the bus conductors and his driver who had started from their garage at 9.0 p.m. The sirens wailed. They decided to keep going. In ten minutes occurred the first incident—in King's Road, Brentwood. A soldier was walking down the middle of it in the direction of Romford. Three bombs fell, one

London Transport enrolled 11,250 clippies. A bus conductor would spend up to a week in the classroom

(above) *—and a week gaining practical experience before she had the knowledge and confidence to* (below) *work on her own.*

on each side of the road and one in the middle. The soldier disappeared—just blown to bits. After sheltering for twenty minutes, the two men decided to carry on. They did so. Another bomb dropped near them on Ongar Road. They decided to take shelter again. More incendiaries and high explosives crashed down. But let the conductor continue in his own words:

'A policeman came down the shelter and told us all to clear out as the shelter was bound to be hit as it seemed to be a sure target. Pointing to the traffic lights on the top of the hill I said to him, "Put that out." He said, "I can't do that." I said, "Yes you can, use your discretion. If you don't put it out I will knock it out." The lights were an obvious landmark on the hill.

'My driver and I eventually decided to leave the shelter and go elsewhere. I then looked out of the door to see if it was safe enough to leave, but it seemed a coincidence every time I looked out there were sixteen red balls coming down from the sky. So we had to stay there.

'It was early next morning that Jerry seemed to come in with his "last knockings". This time he seemed bent on dropping them straight at us—in one straight line for our shelter—they came on and on and on, closer and closer and then—nothing! I was in the front of the shelter with my head and shoulders stuck in the wall. We counted them. One . . . two . . . three . . . seven . . . eight . . . nine . . . we were all going goosey; they were getting closer; we were all going crackers; we knew we were going crackers. I could feel my blinking hat going up and up, my hair was pushing it up, it was standing on end—my head was sticking closer and closer into the wall. We were like lumps of jelly. The bombs had stopped falling—short of reaching the shelter.

'After a time the *All Clear* went and we went out to try and get our bus back to the garage. We had to take a long diversion, and there were heavy oak trees on either side of the lanes we went up. Every time the leaves and branches touched the side of the bus—and we were going some pace—I went flat on the floor of the bus. I thought it was bombs coming at us!

'We kept going until at last we had to pull up because there was a shelter blown clean out of the ground on to the centre of the roadway. We investigated and found there had been men, women and children in it. All were dead. The house to which it belonged was still standing, quite undamaged.'

Or again, a Building Department man:

'When we were at Camberwell Garage there was bomb damage there and Jerry was knocking it down quicker than we could put it up. There was a lot of damage at the Divisional Office and one Saturday night he hopped over and dropped two bombs on the garage. One fell on the entrance and one in the garage. The one in the garage blew up and a double-decker went up through the roof and a single-decker stood there. All the stanchions came down just as if they had been cut from underneath. The whole roof fell down.

'This left a delayed-action bomb in one of the entrances to the garage. It was a pretty big bomb and they brought the R.E. men down. The lieutenant looked at the bomb and the building and said, "No thank you. This is too risky. If we take that bomb out, the building will fall on us." I said, "Well, take the building down—it's nearly falling down." He said, "No thank you. I prefer the bomb to the building." I said, "Well, I suppose we will have to take the building down."

'I phoned my department and they came to look at it. They left it to me to get the building down. It was hanging out towards the road. The gables were all leaning and the girders resting against it. I decided that if we pulled the building inwards, it would not fall on the bomb. I also arranged with the lieutenant that, if we pulled the building down, he would deal with the bomb.

'We put some boards across the crater where the bomb was and put a ladder on the boards against the brickwork and put a chain round the girder and the brickwork. The police came down and cleared the road, and the garage, and the people out of the places near, and we pulled it down on the chain tackle. All the dust and bricks flew about and the people thought the bomb had gone off and started to come up the road. I got a piece of iron and chalked on it: *This bomb has not gone off.* I put it near the crater. Everybody looked at me and said, "What a liar! He would not be standing there if it had not gone off."

'Then I thought that we were going to have some bad luck. They sent down a corporal and three men, and *they were all cross-eyed*. They were going to take the bomb out. They started to dig for this bomb. They opened the ground out wider and started to cut steps in the side of the clay, looking for the bomb which had not gone off.

'We lent them a ladder—they only had buckets and shovels and a piece of string. Yes, they were badly equipped, and I asked one of them how they came to volunteer for this job. He said, "An officer looked into the hut and said, 'You and you and you on bomb squad'." And he got 2s. 6d. a day for this. Well, they blew the bomb up and though the officer thought that the explosion would blow down all the buildings, even the glass was still in.'

One of the railway permanent way inspectors, on duty at Baker Street, was sent to Whitechapel, where a gang of men were

Passengers and crew were in a shelter when this bus was hit. (Below) *A trolleybus returns to the depot.*

already attempting to clear the debris from the tunnel of the East London line which had been bombed three hours previously. The bomb having passed through a bacon factory, came through the side of the tunnel between Whitechapel and Shoreditch. There was no loss of life. On the contrary, legs of pork ready for curing came down into the tunnel from the bacon factory. . . .

By the dawn of September 8 it was possible to survey the damage as it affected the Board. The garage at Athol Street, Poplar, near Blackwall Tunnel, was completely cut off from supplies of electricity, gas and water, and its windows were broken. All buses were held up when attempting to enter or leave it. Drivers, inspectors and conductors were injured by glass. A few omnibuses had their windows and windscreens damaged, but apart from dozens of diversions made necessary by the bombs which had fallen in twenty-one different parts of London, particularly in the Woolwich area, surprisingly little damage was done; though one passenger was killed and several others injured when a No. 2 bus suffered a near miss from a bomb at Victoria Station. There was, of course, any amount of delay and loss of mileage among the trams and buses.

During the air raid on the following day, two omnibuses were completely blown up, two more were wrecked, another was burnt out and ten more had their windows broken. Another was damaged by machine-gun bullets. Whitechapel Station was damaged by a bomb. The District Line trains were blocked at Wimbledon. Overhead wires were destroyed at Mile End, Commercial Road and Leytonstone among other places. The escalator at Monument was damaged by a high explosive. So was the station at Baker Street, and a bomb near Mornington Crescent Station damaged the Northern Line tunnel.

On September 9, one tram was overturned, several others were damaged and de-railed, and buses normally using London Bridge, Tower Bridge and Southwark Bridge had to be diverted over Blackfriars Bridge. This diversion needs explaining.

Special officials were detailed to do reconnaissances during and after air raids in order to see what routes were out of commission and which would have to be selected to get all essential services running again as soon as possible at dawn. Both the City Police and the Metropolitan Police were exceedingly helpful and in many cases left it to the Board's superintendents to advise which routes were most practical.

On one famous occasion (of which later) it was necessary to divert omnibuses down Old Jewry, a thoroughfare so narrow that there was no room for even a cyclist to pass the vehicle. Omnibuses had to take the most peculiar routes, passing through alleyways which had never seen anything bigger than a donkey shay.

Trolleybuses also had to make astonishing journeys. On one occasion there was a large

The producer-gas bus; 160 of this type were in service, but they were not entirely successful and were withdrawn as soon as the war situation improved. (See p. 25.)

crater in a narrow lane at West Ham off Plaistow High Street. The Board's inspector measured the distance between the edge of the crater and the road and decided that it was just wide enough to permit a trolleybus to pass. He then went to the nearest policeman and said, with old-world courtesy, 'I would be much obliged if you would give me permission to get my service running normally. To prove it, I will get a trolleybus out and measure it.'

The constable replied, 'No, Alf, you ought to know the width of your trolleybuses.'

The inspector promptly telephoned the control room with the news that he had permission to maintain the service through Plaistow. On his return, however, another policeman awaited him. 'Come on, I want you,' he said, and led the inspector back to the bomb crater. 'Who gave you permission to run your trolleybuses over here?' he asked. For there, underneath the part of the lane where the inspector had decided to run his trolleybus, was a huge arch traverse which would have collapsed in a moment under the weight of an omnibus. But it was only 2.0 a.m. and the inspector still had time to arrange another diversion.

He, like other trolleybus inspectors, had to walk as much as four miles a night through roads to inspect the overhead wires as well as the bomb craters on the route. Many a time they did not go to bed until 9.0 a.m. to make sure that the drivers did not take the wrong turnings and find themselves in a cul-de-sac. Equally, they had to carry torches and signal the drivers of on-coming omnibuses and trolleybuses on the early shift, who were gallantly nosing their way through the blackout without any real foreknowledge of the diversions ahead of them. Often it happened that bombs would drop and make roads impassable only a few minutes after the inspectors had nominated some particular road as practical. Which meant that, once again, they had to risk the falling buildings, the showers of glass, the incendiaries, the bombs and the shrapnel, to make sure that the services were once again ready for the early-morning workers.

The linesmen (the men who put up the trolley wires) were equally conscientious and just as brave. As often as not they were on the scene of an incident before the A.R.P., because they knew immediately from the interruption of the electric circuit when something had happened. There were twenty-four crews of mate, linesman and driver per tower-wagon, with three shifts per 24 hours. This meant that 216 men were responsible for maintaining the overhead sections of trolleybuses throughout London. The various crews were stationed at strategic positions. Sometimes it was necessary for them to assist in moving casualties, as well as debris, in order to get on with the job. On one occasion men were already working when an explosion occurred in the blackout and, having turned the searchlight on their tower-wagon on to the blitzed building, they rescued the survivors.

Normally, however, they left it to the A.R.P. to deal with casualties, while they hurriedly but efficiently restored the overhead lines to enable the trolleybuses to operate again as soon as possible. The average length of time between taking over a job by the linesmen and the renewal of the trolleybus service was four hours, irrespective of the length of the overhead wire which had to be replaced. The replacing of the wires—which were half an inch thick and weighed half a pound per foot—also necessitated temporary supports. The usual distance which separates supporting poles is forty yards. Fortunately, however, it was very seldom that the blast would knock down all the poles supporting the wire which had been brought to the ground. In any event it was possible, temporarily, to bridge the gaps of blitzed poles by mechanical means.

Each tower-wagon carried a telescopic tower from which the linesmen were able to reach the level of the wire and here, perched precariously some 20 feet above the ground, they repaired the overhead wires oblivious of the blitz around them. For, though some men felt their position keenly, the majority were so busy on the job that their intense activity took their minds off their extremely dangerous position. Nevertheless, it must have been a most unpleasant, naked feeling to be on the top of a tower-wagon in the middle of an air raid, with H.E., incendiaries and shrapnel falling all around. But, no matter how fierce the bombing might be, the linesmen never ceased until they had completed their job, sometimes working consecutively for eighteen hours. All agreed that the best repair job was near a fire, as often happened. They said that the sound of the N.F.S. pump drowned the noise of the gunfire and the bombs. What is more, they kept warm as well. This was a real consideration, for during the bitter winter of 1940-41 the repairing of overhead wires, frequently during snow storms, was no picnic.

On many occasions, of course, the overhead linesmen would arrive on the scene of an incident and would find that the crater in the road was so immense that it would have been a sheer waste of time to repair the wires. Whereupon they retired disconsolately until instructions were received from Head Office. These instructions invariably involved diversions. Diversions in turn involved a great deal of strenuous work. When, for example, a diversion at Green Street, Upton Park, was extended to a quarter of a mile, it was necessary to dig twenty-two holes, six feet deep, through the pavement, to carry the poles which in turn were to carry the overhead wires.

Long before the end of the war scores of miles of overhead wire had been substituted as a result of the blitz and hundreds of poles replaced. In the northern division alone, 560 incidents were successfully tackled.

5

Live, Delayed-action or Dud?

A s t h e raids increased, the work of the Permanent Way Department became more hectic. The railway emergency headquarters was at Chalk Farm and on the receipt of urgent messages from the A.R.P. authorities via Railway Control, or from actual members of the staff who had found unexploded bombs on railway property, the officer on duty immediately imposed temporary restrictions before hurrying down to the incident. These temporary restrictions were: (1) the complete closing of the line, (2) the working of a single line, or (3) the limitation of speed to 5 m.p.h.

Parking in the park. Permission was obtained for buses and trolleybuses to wait in Regent's Park, on Victoria Embankment and other places until required in the peak hours, instead of going home. This saved more than two million miles a year.

Many of the unexploded bombs were in most awkward positions. The officer on duty might be able to walk along the track from the nearest station. But as often as not the quickest method was to drive to the nearest point, jump over the fence or climb the bridge to make a personal reconnaissance and establish whether it was indeed an unexploded bomb, and to determine the possible extent of the damage.

This identification demanded great knowledge and experience. The bombs might be anything from 100–1,000 lb. They might be delayed-action. There was also the question of whether they were armour-piercing or the blast-effect type. In addition there were 500 and 1,000 lb. oil bombs, photographic bombs and various types of incendiary canisters.

It was soon discovered that of every thousand bombs dropped, about a hundred were delayed action, while many of the 500 lb. delayed-action category were duds.

At the start there were a number of false alarms. Out of an average of fifteen messages, five would be based on false reports, another five would concern genuine unexploded

TRAVEL INFORMATION
SUBURBAN RAILWAYS   LONDON TRANSPORT

S
HERE

One result of dislocations and diversions to traffic was the demand for up-to-date information. In conjunction with the Main Line Railways London Transport set up and manned 23 kiosks at strategic points in the City and West End. In one week more than 100,000 inquiries were answered.

bombs which did not, however, affect the Board's railway system. The remaining five would be the genuine article. Of these, a high proportion were usually duds.

Unexploded bombs which fell on the open railway track or alongside it were not so tricky to handle as those that were located in buildings. Experience showed that the life of a delayed-action fuse was seldom more than ninety-six hours and that it was never timed to explode in under three hours (otherwise it would not have been a genuine delayed-action bomb). The patrols, who worked in pairs, were therefore comparatively safe if they were quick on the job.

During this phase a bomb was suspected of having caused track damage somewhere inside the triangle of Hounslow, Acton Town and South Harrow, because of the loss of current. Eventually it was located near Alperton because it was found that certain railway telephones were not operating. A squad was rushed by lorry to Park Royal Station. Here they set out along the track through the blackout. The leading man practically fell into the crater a few hundred yards away. Over eighty feet of track had been blown away. The remaining lines were wildly distorted. Cables and air mains had been severed. There was a hole in the bank extending on to the track itself, the actual cra-

ter being fifty feet across and twenty feet deep.

While the permanent-way men, by the light of their hooded flare lamps, straightened out the distorted track and started to fill the crater, an emergency train filled with sleepers, new rails and ballast, crawled up to the nearest available point. By noon the trains were running again.

On hundreds of occasions bomb damage caused to the permanent way was repaired before the first train ran next morning, and the public never knew what had happened.

One eerie dawn the official on duty received an urgent message to say that an unexploded bomb was believed to have fallen in Victoria Street, possibly in the basement of a house near the Board's tunnel. He dashed to the scene, found the area roped off by the police and realised instantly that the bomb, if any, would be practically on top of the precious tunnel. He produced his pass, entered the blitzed building, rummaged around by the light of his torch to find the path of the bomb, discovered a hole in the ground floor, looked upwards and saw the corresponding hole in the roof, struggled down through the rubble into the basement and suddenly found it at his very feet.

There it was, a thousand-pound bomb, lying on its side, greenish-grey, monstrous. How close was the tunnel? He scraped at the debris and realised with a shock that it was only eight yards away. He put his ear as close to it as possible. It sounded like a lady's wrist-watch, very faint. Or was it his imagination?

He had already given temporary instructions for the tunnel to be put out of operation. He now hurried out to the police barrier and telephoned the military bomb-disposal headquarters at Chelsea as well as Railway Control. He returned to the bomb with a young sapper officer, showed him the bomb.

'Can you hear it ticking?' he asked.

'Let's see.'

The officer scraped round the bomb to locate the exact position of the fuse head, found it and announced that it was so far underneath that he would need a mirror to identify its type.

The Board's man, thereupon hurried off to the barrier, where he saw a pretty girl. 'Lend me your mirror, miss,' he begged.

'What for?' she asked.

'Never mind, I'll bring it back to you.'

He returned for the third time to the ticking monster. The sapper edged the mirror under the bomb. Yes, it was definitely a time fuse, category A. This was top priority.

The Board's man again left the bomb and returned with a brigadier armed with a stethoscope. By this time he felt that he had seen quite enough of the bomb. The brigadier duly stethoscoped it, like a doctor testing the heart-beat of a child. He confirmed the previous diagnosis.

The question now was—would the railway tunnel cave in? The official thought that it would not do so. The brigadier said firmly that the bomb was to be left severely alone . . .

Three hours later it exploded with a prodigious roar, completely demolishing the building but not affecting the tunnel.

As more factories and docks were bombed and damaged and workers had to be transferred, the Board was asked by the Government to run a service of boats between Westminster and Woolwich. On the day before it started there had been a particularly serious disruption of transport facilities. Six sub-stations had been put out of action by the fracture of main cables from Greenwich. Streatham and New Cross Depots had been hit. Practically the whole of the East Ham and West Ham trolleybus services were out of action. The whole of central (south) and practically all south-east London, together with parts of south-west London and central (north), were without trams and trolleybuses owing to unexploded bombs, though petrol buses did their best to cover the area.

For the river service, fifteen boats and tugs were used, the Port of London Authority providing the boats, crews and stores, while the Board arranged the supply of inspectors and conductors. The piers of call were Westminster, Tower Bridge, Cherry Garden, Tunnel, South-West India Dock, Greenwich,

Anchors aweigh at Westminster.

Brunswick and North Woolwich. The approximate interval between boats was half an hour on weekdays and sixty minutes on Sundays, the purpose being to cater for the various factories and wharves in Greenwich and Woolwich. Unfortunately the running-time between Westminster and North Woolwich was over two hours, double that taken by trams, and the service was twice interrupted by mines in the Thames. So it was withdrawn in six weeks.

On land, dangerous buildings, fire-hoses over the tracks and barrage balloon cables across the overhead wires, added to the difficulties of the trolleybuses. On September 16 there were no fewer than five air raids, the last being infinitely the most severe. Bombs in Bond Street and Park Lane caused many diversions. Several buses were required to help passengers on all the main railway systems.

At dawn on September 19 it was impossible to contact either the southern, south-western, north-western or north-eastern areas by telephone. Oxford Street, from Marble Arch to Oxford Circus, was closed. So was the whole of Wigmore Street. Forty buses at Catford Garage alone had been damaged. Bombs had fallen elsewhere at Balham, St. Pancras, Marylebone Road (outside Regents Park Underground Station) and in Regent Street near Piccadilly Circus. Communications had, in many cases, to be maintained by motor cycle despatch riders.

A cheque in payment for the first of two London Transport Spitfires given by the staff was handed over to the Minister of Aircraft Production in 1942. A second followed nine months later. The aircraft carried the London Transport bullseye symbol into a new element.

6 Underground Nights: at Home in the Tube

So IT WENT on. Day after day, night after night, bombs fell all over London. No wonder that the crowds in the Tube shelters increased, in spite of the incidents near the Marble Arch and Tottenham Court Road shelters. No fewer than 177,000 people were recorded as having taken shelter from the blitz in the Tubes on September 27, 1940. But later on, familiarity with the Luftwaffe's raids bred a growing contempt and the average numbers of shelterers dwindled thereafter until they were temporarily stabilised at about sixty thousand per night. (Even on VE-night there were still twelve thousand squatters on the Underground Tube stations and in the deep shelters.)

In all, seventy-nine stations were used by shelterers in Greater London. In addition, some miles of Tube tunnel, either temporarily disused (such as the Aldwych branch), or not yet used, as in the case of the eastern extension of the Central Line through Bethnal Green, West Ham, Leyton and Leytonstone, also provided protection. A number of disused stations like British Museum, City Road, and South Kentish Town were, as already mentioned, handed over to the local authorities for whom the Board's workmen prepared them for occupation.

These were naturally more popular than the ordinary public shelters owing to their relative degree of safety, spaciousness, good lighting, ventilation and improved sanitary arrangements. Further, both bombs and gunfire were inaudible. The common sense of the public was ultimately proved by the fact that throughout the various blitzes there were astonishingly few incidents at Tube stations which had fatal results, and none of these occurred after the first five months of the blitz.

Improvised lavatory accommodation for men and women, together with medical-aid posts were erected with exemplary promptitude by the Board's staff at all stations. These improvisations were quickly replaced, however, by permanent arrangements, at a cost of many thousands of pounds, and five special shelter inspectors were appointed to ensure that cleanliness and hygiene was maintained. Soon, too, a refreshment service was operated. The food included meat pies, pasties, sausage rolls, apple turnovers, cakes and buns. As much as seven tons of food and 2,400 gallons of liquid such as tea, cocoa and milk were sold nightly.

With the advice and approval of the Ministry of Health and Lord Horder, modern medical-aid posts with at least one fully-trained nurse and in some instances full-time doctors, were installed at every station. Altogether there were thirty doctors and two hundred nurses engaged in this work. Many shelterers used them like an ordinary hospital out-patients' department, to obtain treatment for minor ailments which had nothing to do with the blitz. Fortunately infection

The Welfare organisation fed 120,000 shelterers each night.

among the shelterers was insignificant—a proportion of one case per five thousand persons —immunisation against diphtheria, and throat spraying against other infectious diseases being made simple by the local authorities.

Soon, enough bunks to accommodate over 22,000 people were installed. Unfortunately, the prototypes supplied by the Home Office were a wooden structure, and therefore highly vulnerable to vermin. It was not until later that they could be exchanged for steel structures. In the meantime it was necessary to have special squads of men to keep parasites under control.

The reason for not supplying more bunks was psychological. Whilst families appreciated them, other people preferred separate places on the platform, and, at two stations where bunks had been fixed, requests were actually made for their removal. During that grim autumn and winter of 1940, shelterers arrived between 5.0 p.m. and 6.0 p.m. but showed no inclination to sleep before 10.0 p.m. They occupied the intervening period by talking with their friends, having refreshments with them, playing cards and even chess. None of this cheerful communal life would have been possible if all available space had been occupied by bunks.

One important aspect of this strange troglodyte existence was provided by the need for the allocation of accommodation. Generally speaking it was arranged that six people should occupy six feet of platform length— three sleeping in a bunk and three on the platform in front of it. Notting Hill Gate Station was the pioneer of this scheme. Then a standard reservation ticket, printed by the Board, was issued by the local authorities to each shelterer. The ticket bore a number corresponding to a platform position, the same type of ticket being used for either bunk or floor space. In addition, an average of ten per cent of the total accommodation at each station was kept free for casual shelterers, and a blue casual ticket was issued for this purpose. Naturally, no charge was made to shelterers to enter the stations.

This system guaranteed an orderly movement in and out of stations, which meant that members of the public could arrive at varying times during the night, and yet be sure of accommodation. Previously, pathetic queues of women and children had formed outside the stations, some as early as 10.0 a.m. although nobody was allowed to shelter in the stations before 4.0 p.m. The invariable practice was for parents to send their children in advance with the family bedding to take their place in the queue, often in bitter weather.

Then shelterers complained of the difficulty of getting to sleep under the glare of the station lighting. Instructions were therefore given for it to be reduced as far as possible after traffic hours, except in the corridors and subways, where there had to be enough lighting to permit of proper supervision and to ensure safety. All lighting was fully restored before the shelterers began to leave in the morning. Every platform was supplied with hurricane-lamps in case the electricity failed, and in addition to the voluntary shelter marshals, one paid warden was posted to each station.

Looking back on it all, it is astonishing to what lengths the Board went to make life more comfortable for the unfortunate shelterers—fifty-two lending libraries, programmes of gramophone music (and for Christmas over eleven thousand toys were distributed to child shelterers between the ages of three and fifteen). At Elephant & Castle and at Gloucester Road, play centres and educational centres with qualified teachers to organise handicrafts were provided for the children who averaged one to every eight adults. Cans for drinking water, even drinking fountains, notice boards on which special announcements were exhibited, portable hand-washing basins and automatic cigarette machines were provided. So was storage accommodation for the many shelterers who originally left their bedding at the stations during the day, thereby causing a risk of fire and giving rise to complaints from ordinary passengers. Best of all, a special sleeping-bag was made for the shelterers with a damp-proof rexine bag and a blanket attached.

Everybody who has travelled on the Underground realises that dust and draughts are inevitable in the Tubes. Experiments were therefore carried out to spray the air and thus counteract the effect of any possible airborne diseases. Complaints during the cold weather of severe draughts caused by the station ventilation fans were met by stopping them from 9.0 p.m. to 6.0 a.m. at a number of stations, though they were reinstated when the warm weather returned.

Another problem was provided by mosquitoes which failed to hibernate. A squad of ten experts proceeded to deal with them successfully.

The total length of platforms and subways used by shelterers, together with the total length of tunnels east of Liverpool Street and the Aldwych branch, reached a figure of fifteen miles, equivalent to the distance from Hyde Park Corner to Ruislip Manor. Yet only one fatal accident occurred—when a shelterer fell on the running track in front of a train at Shepherds Bush.

In respect of the other accidents, only ten claims for damage were received, of which eight were repudiated—showing that they were evidently caused by negligence on the part of the shelterers themselves. Of the two claims where payment was made, one concerned a shelterer who swallowed a drawing-pin in a bun. The other was for an asthma inhaler broken in a man's pocket because the escalator, on which he was resting, was restarted without warning.

No wonder that the general morale of the shelterers remained at a high level. During raids when local shelters had been bombed, the shelterers came to the stations without

A cloakroom for bedding—a much-appreciated service for the 'regular'. Things might have been worse, there was warmth and light, companionship and food—

—and if things went wrong (above) *you could be sure of sympathy and help and* (below), *most important, there was sleep for the weary.*

showing any of the distress which might have been expected in people whose homes had gone. At London Bridge Station alone, there were 134 families without homes—in all 350 people who, if not at work, remained with sympathetic friends during the day before returning to the station at night. Panic was shown on one occasion only, and this occurred in a party of foreigners who became scared when the tunnel roof was breached and, running towards the exit, fell over shelterers in the dim light then prevailing. The Londoners moved from the platforms to the exits in an orderly manner.

In a very short time the shelterers were enjoying a relatively-speaking comfortable existence. Living was cheap. They were saving money on electric light and other overheads which would have affected their income if they had stayed at home. They were being served cups of tea, jam rolls, meat pies, chocolate biscuits and various sorts of sandwiches. True, there was a certain amount of discomfort caused by fellow-shelterers who kept on talking until they were silenced. But on the whole, life in the shelters was by no means unpleasant, and remarkably safe.

Some of the committees formed of people who took refuge in certain London stations actually produced local newspapers. Among these was *The Swiss Cottager*, which addressed itself to 'nightly companions, temporary cave-dwellers, sleeping companions, somnambulists, snorers, chatterers and all who inhabit the Swiss Cottage Station of the Bakerloo Line from dusk to dawn'. The first issue thanked the Board for allowing the use of the station as a whole, and the station-master and his staff for their help. Injunctions to shelterers included a request to refrain from taking up too much room, to leave no litter, to suffer a little inconvenience to make room for the next person, and to respect the white line.

This referred to an official notice issued by the Board, insisting that passengers should be allowed free and uninterrupted use of platforms and stations, for which purpose two white lines were marked on each station platform, one four feet and the other eight feet from the edge of the platform. Between 4.0 p.m. and 7.30 p.m. sheltering was only allowed between the platform wall and the white line furthest from the platform edge, though after 7.30 p.m. the space between the wall and the line nearest the edge of the platform was also available. Nobody was allowed to shelter in any passageway before 7.30 p.m. except in large circulating areas where a portion was marked off for this purpose.

The paramount need for issuing numbered tickets corresponding to platform space had been exposed by organised gangs who had taken pitiless advantage of the public by demanding as much as half-a-crown for platform space. This they had personally reserved before noon with bunches of ill-favoured rags to represent the bedding normally used by shelterers to stake their claims to a particular spot. These racketeers had previously made a livelihood out of reserving stools in theatre queues, but as the theatres had been officially closed they had turned their attention to the shelterers, already victimised by children who had not, however, the courage to charge more than 4d. for similar reservations. The Board did its best to suppress this nuisance. Within a month of the arrival of the squatters, nobody was allowed to take shelter in the Tubes before 4.0 p.m.

It will be remembered, of course, that even the Tubes were not entirely immune from the Luftwaffe. Seven shelterers were killed when Trafalgar Square Station was hit. On the following night nineteen were killed at Bounds Green Station.

The word went quickly round that the station had been hit, but this is the first account ever printed of the incident.

The Board's first report to the Railway Executive Committee stated briefly:

'At Praed Street Station three bombs fell on the station and it is believed that eight persons have been killed; the roof, platforms and track have been damaged.

'The most serious damage to railway property last night occurred at Bounds Green when some eight segments were smashed and there was a heavy fall of debris on to the track and platforms at the east end of the west-bound track. Information at present available shows that seven persons were killed and fifty-two injured, and it is feared that there are still more people buried under the debris.'

In fact, nineteen people were killed, all except three of whom were Belgians. A local colony of refugees from Belgium had ensconced themselves at the far end of the west platform on the first night of the blitz. They kept themselves to themselves, and it was only because they had been blitzed out of two homes in the previous forty-eight hours that the foreman ticket-collector had permitted three British subjects to shelter in the Belgians' section of the platform.

The ticket-collector had just made this arrangement when he decided to ascend to ground level and make a personal reconnaissance of the blitz overhead. A solitary German aircraft had been flying round for nearly half an hour, evidently in search of a particular target. As the ticket-collector stared upwards he heard the whizz of a bomb, followed by a crash of glass. The bomb had fallen on the top of four 3-storeyed houses to the right of the station. The ground did not vibrate unduly and he presumed that no particular damage had been done.

However, as he walked down to platform level he heard screaming. Half the platform was in darkness. At the far end he could see that the tunnel had caved in. Having allocated the sleeping accommodation only a few minutes previously, he knew that at least sixty people must be involved. Crowds were milling round the safe section of the platform. He promptly sent a porter to the local A.R.P. headquarters and, himself, hurried to the nearby hospital which provided two doctors and six nurses.

With these reinforcements he returned to the scene and made his way behind the debris where he found fifteen or twenty injured

← (centre pages) *The incident at Bank Station.*

Belgians. These were removed to hospital. In the meantime volunteers from Wood Green trolleybus depot hurried over in their lorry to lend further aid. Drivers, conductors and engineers, armed with picks, shovels and other A.R.P. equipment rendered invaluable service in digging out the casualties, although technically it was no affair of theirs.

By 3.0 a.m. all the injured people had been taken away, but nearly a week elapsed before all the corpses had been removed.

The British survivors showed no signs of panic. On the contrary, one old lady commented, 'We'll sleep well tonight. At least there'll be no more trains coming through.' Others asked whether they could come down the following evening, being afraid that the station would be closed. In fact, rail traffic was impossible for two months, but the Tube station kept open for the shelterers.

On the following night an even worse disaster occurred when Balham Station received a direct hit and no fewer than sixty-four shelterers were killed.

The scene was a shambles. The bomb fell into the middle of the roadway, penetrating the north-bound station tunnel and causing the whole length of the station platform to be buried under gravel and sand. Water from burst mains and sewers flooded both tunnels and both sides of the station. The emergency portable pumps were not powerful enough to deal with the flood, and assistance had to be obtained from the London Fire Service. Ultimately seven million gallons of water had to be drained off to enable the trains from Morden to reach the scene and start clearing the debris.

There were about six hundred people sheltering on the station, when a terrific crash was heard, the platform shook and the lights went out. Almost immediately water started to trickle through. Within five minutes it was like a strong flowing river, three feet deep, bringing tons of sand and rubble with it. There was a grim stench of gas.

Here is the unvarnished account of one of the survivors—a motorman employed by the Board:

'It was about 8.0 p.m. I was standing on the platform talking to people when there was a terrific explosion above the station and, at the same time one of the platform lamps "arced", and that put the station in darkness. When the station went into darkness panic started; it was bad panic. I said to them, "It will be all right; we will have a light on in a few moments."

'There were a lot of women and children including my wife and two children and I was talking to them. When I was saying we could soon get a light, I didn't realise that the tunnel had collapsed. Then there was a smell of gas and the children were shouting out for their gas masks. I got my torch and I flashed it up and saw water was pouring down in torrents.

'I thought it was time something was done to get these people out. I went back and opened the emergency hatch. I got the people more disciplined and they filed through the escape hatch in single file. It took about ten minutes to pass them through the hatch—about seventy or eighty of them. I told them to come up the escalator to wait in the booking hall, and the rescue squad came along and took my torch and I had to manage without one.

'All this time water was pouring in and I was up to my knees in water. Soon it was like a waterfall. In about five minutes all the anti-suicide pits were full. The water went up to about the second stair of the escalator.'

The motorman still has scars on his hands caused by people tearing at them whilst he was trying to draw the bolts of the emergency hatch.

Up above, an omnibus was being driven gallantly through the blitz towards Vauxhall, in spite of eight 'chandeliers' hanging immediately overhead. As it reached Balham High Road, the bomb fell barely twenty-five yards ahead. Let the driver tell his own story.

'My bus began prancing about like a horse and the next thing I knew was that I was lying in a shop doorway. I picked myself up and was taken to Ducane Road for first aid. My conductor had been laid out. Apparently he had flung himself on the floor of the bus as I braked and so consequently was concussed.

'He has since enlisted in the army.

'After leaving the first-aid post I decided I must go back to the bus, but as I approached it I said to myself, "It's O.K., somebody's moved it." But when I came nearer I saw to my horror that only the roof was protruding from the crater in the road.'

Wars cannot prevent Christmas—wherever there are children.

Here is another survivor's story of the same incident:

'I climbed up the ballast, which was seeping through the emergency exit on to the platform (I sank into it). I crawled through the emergency exit and shone my torch and had a shock when I saw a mountain of ballast, sand and water washing through a huge hole at the north end of the platform. The emergency exit is very small—you have to stoop to get through it.

'The water was about two feet deep in the lower booking hall. I crossed it and went through the emergency exit at an angle, crawling up the ballast. Very noisy it was, with a hissing of gas and water washing down. As it poured through the tunnel, it washed past me like a river, from right to left. It was like the sand and pebbles at Brighton on a very rough day.

'I shone the torch and had a bit of a shock. I called at the top of my voice to see if anybody was there, but could not hear any sound except the rushing water and hissing. It was gradually filling up. It was about twenty feet in a gradual slope straight down the length of the station. The people were trapped directly beneath the slope, the heap of ballast near the emergency exit. The bomb had brought all the earth down on the inter-passage. The emergency exit was on the north platform. The station master's office was just behind the cross-passage. The station master was killed.

'Four of the police decided to go up the escalator and see what they could do there, and I, the Divisional Traffic Inspector and two policemen decided to go back through the tunnel to Clapham South in case anybody was in the tunnels.

'We stepped down again and this time the water was much deeper. I did not worry because I can swim. I went first, then the two police, and then the Divisional Traffic Inspector followed. The police were told to follow directly behind me and step over trips and manhole covers. It got deeper and deeper and we were pushing against the water.

'We came to a bolt-hole from the northbound to the southbound and the water was rushing through there. It nearly pushed you over. I could not see any lighting and it was getting deeper. Then one of the policemen got his foot jammed in a check rail. We had to get his foot out. Although it was only a couple of minutes, it seemed about ten. I told him to be careful and keep behind me, as he was holding up the troops.

'It was still getting deeper. I could then see the reflection of the lights from Clapham South, but we had not reached the deepest point. I went on in front of the others and the water was above my waist. As I got to the bend of the tunnel, I could see in the distance—half a mile away—the water was flattening out, and I thought we could make it. I called to the two policemen to hurry along as we

were O.K. if we could get through now. We got to the deepest point, which was then chest-high, and got on the upward grade and on our way to Clapham South.

'By this time, in the deepest point, the water was about to touch the tunnel lights, which would have caused a short and put out all the lights. We had a double race—to beat the water and the going out of the lights. We got through back to Clapham South and about half an hour afterwards the tunnel filled up. Then they (the engineers) debated whether to seal the tunnel off.

'We must hand it to the rescue people who came there. They did a wonderful job and started to bring out the bodies between three and four in the morning.

'I had a horrible task to identify the bodies. After a night like that, it was not too good when it was our own staff we had to identify. There was the station-master, a couple of porters, a booking clerk and his family. We got them out from the station-master's office. The rescue people went down the southbound tunnel, through the bolt-hole, and came down through the back. They had to carry all the bodies quite a way and they worked very hard. There were two men to each stretcher and a man guiding them. They looked thoroughly tired out.

'I myself had a headache for a week afterwards because of the gas.'

These and other incidents called for immediate repair-work in order to get trains running again as soon as possible. The removal of damaged rolling-stock was at least as arduous as the towing away of road vehicles. Seven breakdown lorries and a complete breakdown train were utilised for this essential service. The train was based on Neasden which also had two breakdown lorries with their crews of five to seven men. Two other crews and lorries were based on Golders Green and Wood Lane. The seventh was at Morden.

The majority of the work was done by the lorries. To begin with, the breakdown train could not work on the Tube system. And it frequently happened that the rail track was cut between Neasden and the scene of the incident. But when the breakdown train came into action, as it did on a dozen major occasions, it did yeoman service, particularly at Farringdon Street to which it was rushed on four separate occasions to remove damaged railway coaches which weighed anything from twenty-eight to sixty tons.

The very first night of the blitz on London (September 7, 1940), the breakdown lorries went into action at Plaistow, where a bomb threw a thirty-five ton coach on top of another. That night five trains were immobilised within an area of one mile, but in each instance the site was clear for traffic within twenty-four hours. The Plaistow railway coach had to be sliced into pieces, each weighing about a hundredweight, with acetylene cutters while the bombs were still falling. On another occasion the breakdown lorry crews arrived to find a train at Moorgate on fire. The heat was so terrific that the glass and aluminium doors had dissolved into molten pools.

At another incident, six railway coaches were pulled away by means of a 120 foot steel hawser. Time and again the men had to be lowered to the scene of the wreckage by means of ladders or buckets lowered by crane, there being no other access to the site.

Many times work had to be carried out in two or three feet of water flowing out of broken tanks. By contrast, work often had to be done by the light of blazing gas mains.

On one occasion a breakdown engineer, hurrying to the scene of disaster, had to drive his private car along the pavement of New Oxford Street, dodging round pillar boxes and lamp-posts to avoid the craters in the road. On another appalling night six major jobs—at Kings Cross, Bow Road, Baker Street, London Road, Neasden and Aldgate —were cleared in twenty-four hours. At Colindale, flames shot 270 feet into the air as the men cleared the track. At Southfields, sixty-five tons of concrete had fallen on a train and had to be manhandled away so that the track could be cleared within twenty-four hours. Unexploded bombs, bulging walls and buildings on fire added to the dangers and difficulties.

Sometimes freak blast would cause the

Almost a routine job. A few hundred tons . . . quite straightforward

After the fire at Moorgate Station.

roof of a railway coach to bulge upwards—above the level of the tunnel roof. On such occasions it was necessary to 'squeeze' it into a comparatively normal shape so that it could negotiate the journey in safety.

Primarily the job of these breakdown lorry crews was to remove damaged rolling-stock so that the lines would be clear for traffic as soon as possible, and this involved (a) the removal of debris in the immediate neighbourhood of the track, (b) the cutting away of anything which could fall on the track, and (c) repairing the train sufficiently to enable it to move away under its own power, if this were possible.

But tribute must also be paid to the men in the workshops who made the damaged rolling-stock fit for use again. A classic example is provided by the two more or less undamaged halves of separate railway coaches which were joined together to form one complete unit.

. . . joined to form one complete unit →

A bus-transfusion to stimulate the flow of London's traffic. London Transport was able to return the compliment later, sending 334 buses to Coventry, Bristol, Bradford and even to Scotland.

7 The Provincial Buses answer an Appeal

B Y OCTOBER 17, 1940, so many buses had been blitzed that an S.O.S. for assistance had to be sent to the Ministry of War Transport. This led to the despatch, from every part of England and Scotland, of buses to help. Out of the 472 received within a week, there were ten different makes from fifteen different owners, eighty-two of them being single-deckers.

They were indeed the most diverse collection of road transport passenger vehicles ever assembled at one point—oil engined and petrol engined, single and double deck, black, white, brown, red, green and blue, old and new, good and bad—so they came. Hardly a couple were alike, and they all varied in seating capacity, destination blinds and drivers' controls. They came from as far north as Inverness and Aberdeen, from as far west as Exeter and Plymouth. The first of these 'provincials' arrived from Halifax. Good old Yorkshire!

Immediately the destination blinds, fare boards and running letter slips had to be changed, and the vehicles themselves checked over for equipment. Inventories were prepared immediately and away went the first of them to appear on the streets on October 23, thus taking their turn with London's buses amid the bombs and incendiaries.

Gradually the new-comers were sorted out. Oil-engined ones were segregated. Certain special types were sent to some particular garage here; low-loading double-deckers to a particular garage there; single-decker buses somewhere else. Some only just made the journey to London, and the maintenance men took days to put them into serviceable order. Others went quite well for a few days, and then found the work too hard. Very quickly the garages were inundated with repairs to unfamiliar vehicles for which they had no spare parts. In many cases these had to be made specially at Chiswick.

No sooner had they begun to settle down in London service, when the blitz on Birmingham drew away the best batch which were all exactly similar to one of the Board's standard types. Then Sheffield claimed her buses—again of a type for which Chiswick had spares and which the Board would have liked to keep. Many others departed urgently for Coventry.

The remainder broke down, were repaired, found their way into garages and works for docking and overhaul, and gradually improved to a uniform standard. Then, when most of the difficulties had been overcome, they began to slide away home as local demands for them intensified. Towards the end only a few stragglers remained. Even these finally departed.

To supplement the thinning ranks of the trolleybuses, the Board accepted the offer of the Ministry of Supply to take over forty-three trolleybuses specially built for South Africa. These were six inches wider than the maximum normally allowed in Great Britain, while their weight was a ton over the official maximum. Permission had therefore to be obtained for their use on approved routes.

The men who deserved the greatest recommendation for bravery and devotion to duty were the Board's officials and men who made up night shifts and late-turn shifts. No matter what was falling, they brought back buses from the streets where they had been hurriedly parked by their drivers, so that they could be serviced in the garages the same night. They were the men who saved the buses when incendiaries crashed through the roof and then into the buses themselves. They towed back damaged buses. They worked, often against seemingly impossible odds, amid falling shrapnel and glass, so that all the buses were ready on time for the next day's work.

Similar courage was exhibited by the repair men on the Board's railways, and the men who patrolled the lines. It was they who had to detect and report incidents, including unexploded bombs, which affected the Board's properties. The work was dangerous, tiring and unpleasant, but the men behaved magnificently. On one occasion a bomb fell between two groups of men and within twenty yards of both. Some were killed and others injured. One survivor continued to work, his sole reaction being anxiety about his false teeth which he had lost when the blast from the bomb threw him to the ground.

8   *'Defence in Depth':*
the Government
Shelter

IN OCTOBER, 1940, the Minister of Home Security decided that a comprehensive system of deep-level shelters should be provided against further intensive bombing. London Transport were appointed the Ministry's agents for arranging the construction of eight deep-level shelters with sleeping accommodation for 64,000 people, the cost being borne by the Government.

The original idea was that tunnels should be driven at least sixty feet below the surface in various parts of central London, radiating from disused lift shafts. This was obviously undesirable because access from only one shaft to several tunnels would be inadequate and dangerous, while haphazard creation of tunnels beneath the level of the ground would have interfered with the sewerage and drainage of the capital.

The sites provisionally chosen were submitted to the Home Office and eventually it was decided to have five deep shelters south of the Thames at Clapham South, Clapham Common, Clapham North, Stockwell and Oval, with a similar number north of the river at St. Pauls, Chancery Lane, Goodge Street, Camden Town and Belsize Park.

The original design consisted of two parallel tunnels fourteen hundred feet long, with two levels for bunks. Two separate steel-and-concrete staircases were built inside each shaft to provide separate access to the two levels. This minimised overcrowding at the entrances to the shelters, each of which was designed to protect nine thousand people, whose comfort was further studied by the installation of an electric lift conveying tea, coffee and food.

Construction on the first of these shelters— at Chancery Lane—began on November 7, 1940, though work on the other sites was not

The eight Government shelters together had 64,000 bunks. They were designed for their purpose with all the experience gained from the Tube railways and were unrivalled for safety and comfort.

put in hand until much later. When faced with the realities of the job, the engineers found it necessary to vary considerably from the original scheme. Provision of adequate lavatory accommodation, ventilation, medical posts, wardens' offices, children's playgrounds, fire-extinguishing plant and sewerage ejectors demanded a number of alterations. A whimsical situation arose in connection with the proposed deep shelter at St. Pauls. A special Act of Parliament which prohibited the construction of any more Tubes in the vicinity of the Cathedral was produced, so this particular shelter had to be abandoned. The deep-level shelter at the Oval was also stillborn. There was no objection from the Surrey County Cricket authorities, but so much water was encountered after the working-shafts had been sunk, that it had to be abandoned. This meant that the remaining eight shelters had to be made longer than had been originally planned in order that the sixty-four thousand shelterers envisaged should be suitably accommodated.

No fewer than 120 motor lorries had to be obtained to deal with the excavated material and the carriage of the material necessary to line the tunnels from the stack-yards to the various working shafts. Fortunately, permission was obtained from the Chief Officer of the Parks Department of the L.C.C. and the Bailiff of Parks to use large areas of Clapham Common and Regent's Park to dump the rubble. Economically enough the lorries were bought second-hand, overhauled and finally disposed of in a condition fifty per cent better than when bought.

The eight shelters ultimately constructed were unrivalled for safety and comfort. At first they were used as hostels for troops travelling through London who would otherwise have missed a proper night's rest. Later on they were converted into secret headquarters of hush-hush military departments. How many people know, even now, that General Eisenhower's D-day invasion offices were in a deep shelter?

For this purpose a large proportion of the eight thousand bunks was removed, leaving enough however to sleep the military staff, both men and women. The upper floors of both centre tunnels were converted into office premises. Teleprinters were installed and a special telephone exchange having direct contact with the U.S. was arranged. The offices all had fluorescent lighting and conditioned air.

Many people thought that the deep-level shelters were some hundreds of feet below the level of the ground, but the average was about eighty feet and the deepest was 105 feet.

It was not, however, until the flying-bomb phase that these deep-level shelters came into their own, when thousands of Londoners sought refuge in them. Then—to jump forward to 1945—Clapham, Stockwell and Camden Town were taken over by the War Office to accommodate soldiers on their way through London. Chancery Lane was acquired by the Records Office for the storage of valuable documents, after it had been partially converted to office premises for various Whitehall ministries. Clapham Common was commandeered by the Admiralty for the storage of documents while Clapham North and Belsize Park remained empty.

With regard to the relative depth of penetration of enemy bombs, the deepest was experienced at Eversholt Street, St. Pancras— through forty-seven feet of solid ground. The next deepest was at Holloway—forty-five feet, and the third deepest was at Bounds Green— thirty-two feet.

During October and November, 1940, one body-blow after another was delivered at the Board's services. A glance at the accompanying photographs gives a realistic idea of what the repair gangs had to tackle during these appalling months. Tunnels were breached, electric current was cut off, viaducts were smashed, signal circuits were put out of action, rolling-stock was de-railed, roads were cratered, tram tracks were blown to blazes, omnibuses disintegrated. Many of the repairs involved major engineering works. When, for example, Granville Tunnel between Kings Cross and Farringdon was damaged on October 16, it took nine months of hard work to restore the train service. So many bombs fell continuously between Shoreditch and New Cross on the East London Line, that the train services had to be suspended for months at a time. It was only by a miracle of determination and engineering skill that they were reopened at all during the war. In the case of the bombs on the West London Line, Addison Road was put out of commission except for freight trains and hospital trains until the Rheims surrender.

One of the worse incidents during the winter of 1940 was the direct hit on the new station buildings at Sloane Square. The incident occurred at 10.0 p.m. A train was just leaving the station which was crowded with passengers, and a huge lump of concrete went right through one of the coaches. Casualties numbered seventy-nine. There were three others who were never seen again. Two emergency repair gangs were hastily sent from Neasden, the primary job of the crews being to cut away the steelwork, rails and any other obstruction with their acetylene cutters. As the men got to work, in the flickering light, there were screams from trapped passengers wanting help. The escalators were wrecked. The men worked frantically until nightfall, but services on local sections of the Inner Circle were interrupted for a fortnight.

Sometimes the blast from bursting bombs flung 35-ton train cars into the air as if they had been made of cardboard.

And so it went on—bomb after bomb, repair job after repair job. Nothing could have been more disheartening. Time and again the repairs were almost completed when another incident would occur and undo all the good work. Frequently, though, the sleepless, harried men, toiling in the most uncomfortable and dangerous conditions, had mended the roads, tram tracks and train tracks well enough for the public to know nothing about it next morning.

It was during this phase that not only two hundred of the omnibus drivers and instructors were released by the Army, but also 150 reservists volunteered to drive through the blitz in central London. Others drove firemen all the way to the Midlands, remaining there during the equally unpleasant blitzes in the north.

One of them was picked to drive the Romford firemen to the Manchester blitz. He left Romford at about quarter to four on the afternoon of Christmas Eve, 1940. He took a double-deck bus with orders to drive to Gates Corner and then change over to a coach. He filled up with firemen for Manchester, and started off at about 5.0 p.m. The first stop was at Dunstable, where they pulled up and had a meal. The proprietor of the café asked if they were going to Manchester, and then said to the driver, 'I hope you don't do what the man did yesterday.' 'What was that?' asked the driver, and was told that a driver on the previous day had not got very much farther on the road when he misjudged a bend and pitched all his passengers into a ditch, several of them being killed. That was a good start.

The driver continued the journey, making one or two stops *en route* for a meal and a stretch. Between one and two o'clock in the morning he stopped the bus, as he did not want to take the wrong turning, and there were no direction posts. Then along came a six-wheeler lorry. He asked the way, and was told to follow it. He started to do so, but with his load he could not get sufficient power and speed to keep up with the six-wheeler and watched its rear light getting smaller and smaller until it disappeared altogether. However, not long after, he could see the direction of Manchester by the glow of the fires in the sky. But further difficulties arose, and he could not get through because of the bomb craters in the roadway. Ultimately he took instructions and directions from the Military and arrived safely in Manchester, where he waited for the firemen to return until the following Friday afternoon, reaching Romford at 2.0 a.m. on the Saturday.

9 The Battle of London (i) On the Surface

THEN CAME the fearful night of December 29/30. The skies opened. A deliberate and very-nearly-successful attempt was made to destroy the City of London for ever. So many vivid accounts of that historic night have been printed that no attempt will be made here to describe the appalling scenes while the conflagration was at its height. It is better left to the Board's laconic report to the Railway Executive Committee on December 30:

'As a result of the intense attack last night, traffic conditions in the central London area this morning are bad.

'On the Board's railways the District Line is not operating between St. James Park and Aldgate East; the Northern City Line is closed to traffic as a result of damage at Moorgate Substation: the Central Line is closed between Wood Lane and Queens Road, and the widened lines east of Farringdon are closed. Moorgate, St. Pauls, Farringdon, Mark Lane, Blackfriars, Whitechapel, Aldersgate and Wood Lane are closed, in addition to the section of the Northern Line which has been closed for some weeks. There are no bus services operating through the City area due to fires and to the closing of London Bridge, Blackfriars Bridge, Tower Bridge and Southwark Bridge.

'Tram and trolleybus services are unable to reach their normal terminals at London Docks, the Minories, Moorgate, Holborn and on the City side of Southwark Bridge.

'Damage to the Board's property on the railway and tram and trolleybus services is widespread, the major incidents being as under:

'VICTORIA EMBANKMENT. A bomb has badly damaged the girders over the eastbound District Line track, east of Westminster Station, and a tram on the Embankment had a direct hit with a bomb, killing the conductor and four passengers, and injuring the driver and a number of other passengers; the tram track was damaged and single-line working is in operation.

'BLACKFRIARS STATION. Fires adjacent to the station entrances were brought under control.

'MARK LANE. A number of fires are still burning on the line of the tunnel at Mark Lane and eastwards as far as Minories; it is not possible at present to report the damage to the Board's properties and it is not practicable to run trains owing to the dangerous state of the buildings.

'ALDERSGATE STATION. A train was set on fire west of Aldersgate Station but was subsequently extinguished, with no casualties.

'MOORGATE STATION. Buildings were set on fire adjacent to the line between Moorgate and Aldersgate Station, and these fires subsequently spread to the whole of Moorgate Station, including station premises, substation and relay room. At Aldersgate the fire is at present confined to the station roof, but at the moment it is impossible to report the damage.

'WOOD LANE STATION AND DEPOT. Incendiary bombs in the vicinity of the Depot caused fires in the buildings over the north end of the Depot, which were extinguished during the night.

'A number of minor incidents occurred causing damage to property at Whitechapel Station, at the Board's offices at Cranbourn Chambers, Leicester Square, at London Road Depot, Whitechapel Substation, Elephant & Castle Tramway Substation and South Kensington Station, to a train at Hammersmith, at Bank Station, Bermondsey Tramway Substation, Aldgate East signal cabin, London Bridge Station, and at Camberwell, where three trams were burnt out and a conductor sustained injuries. In addition, damage was done to overhead tram and trolleybus cables at a number of localities.

'The number of buses operating this morning to cover railway and tram and trolleybus dislocated services is 656.

'The flood-gates on the under-river sections were closed at 6.10 p.m. and reopened on the East London Line at 12.31 a.m. and on the Bakerloo and Northern Lines at the commencement of traffic this morning. The gates on the District Line were closed at 6.27 p.m. yesterday and have remained closed.

'The number of shelterers at Tube stations on Saturday night was roundly 89,000, and on Sunday night 101,700.'

No satisfactory explanation has yet been given for the failure of the Luftwaffe to follow up the fire blitz of December 29/30. Thus it was that the Board was able to report twenty-four hours later that 'no fresh damage was caused during this period; there was no enemy activity in the Board's area'.

Make-do-and-mend on the Underground.

The report continued:

'The position on the Board's railways is that the Northern (City) Line was reopened to traffic yesterday and is this morning working normally from Moorgate Station; the District Line is reopened between Charing Cross and Mansion House leaving breaks between Mansion House and Aldgate East; the widened lines east of Farringdon were reopened for goods traffic during yesterday, and Blackfriars and Whitechapel Stations are now open. On the Central Line the service has now been suspended between Wood Lane and Marble Arch, the further suspension from Queens Road to Marble Arch having been made in order to improve the service between Marble Arch and the City. On the Circle Line between Aldersgate and Moorgate there is a long section of dangerous buildings which prevent the operation of trains and which will prevent repairs being undertaken to the tracks until the buildings are made safe.

'On the roads there has been a reasonable improvement in the tram and trolleybus position and services have been resumed over Southwark and Blackfriars Bridges; the normal two-way operation has been resumed on the Victoria Embankment; trolleybus services are using the Holborn Loop and the Minories lay-by; Gardiners Corner to the Minories, the Commercial Road, Commercial Street and Great Eastern Street have been reopened, and normal operations have been resumed in the Dulwich Road and the Harrow Road. It is still not practicable for the trolleybus services to reach the London Docks terminus, Moorgate terminus or to use the section of the Whitechapel Road between Cambridge Road and Commercial Street; Great Dover Street is closed and there are a number of shorter sections of tram and trolleybus routes where services are curtailed. In addition, a fresh outbreak of fire in the Westminster Bridge Road last night has caused a substantial number of diversions of tram routes normally using this thoroughfare on their journeys to Town.

'It has not yet been practicable to resume the operation of bus services through the City and, while Tower Bridge is now being used by buses, London Bridge, Blackfriars Bridge and Southwark Bridge, although open to traffic, cannot be used by normal bus services in view of the condition of the approach roads to these bridges. In the East End, Canning Town Bridge has been reopened and in the West-End the reopening of Charing Cross Road and the section of the Edgware Road has improved the traffic position.

'The number of buses working this morning on special services for railway and tramway passengers is 546.

'The number of shelterers in the Tube stations during the night was 103,600.'

Damage was severe but never crippling. Out of a fleet of 3,869 railway cars, 19 were totally destroyed and 1,050 were hit (including damage inflicted on separate occasions). On buses, trams and trolleybuses the proportion was very much higher.

This unemotional account is exact and precise in its details. It was neither the time nor the place at that moment to pay tribute to the superb work of the Board's men who, by hook or by crook, managed to get so many services in working order so quickly again. The streets of the City looked like plates of spaghetti milanaise—the spaghetti being represented by the thousands of firemen's hoses and the milanaise by the lumps of rubble and concrete from the blitzed buildings.

Amongst it all, the District Superintendent in charge of all City buses worked untiringly and heroically, whilst his son, an inspector, ran the gauntlet of fire after fire in the Dock area to ensure that his beloved omnibuses from Athol Street Garage should keep going.

On one occasion explosive incendiaries showered down on to the latter's office just as two bombs fell in the immediate neighbourhood. He was knocked off his feet, but jumped up just as the walls caved in. Another bomb fell and knocked more walls down. Then the police telephoned to say that they

needed an abandoned omnibus moved in
Cubitt Town because it was causing an obstruction to the firemen. Nobody else was
anxious to go out, so the inspector and his
foreman set off in another bus to tow it back.
Fortunately, as several diversions were necessary, he knew the back streets of the East
End, but just past Charley Brown's in West
India Dock Road, he had to drive literally
through the flames. The bus was located at
Bullivant's Wharf and the inspector duly
drove it back, leaving the foreman to follow
in the other. Next day the few omnibuses that
were serviceable had to be worked on a shuttle service. Diversions were fantastic, and in
many cases the drivers on the early shift were
told to use their own judgment.

Then Blackwall Tunnel was closed by a
land mine on the south side. This was awkward. Blackwall Tunnel, having been originally designed for horse traffic only, had required the building of thirty specially shaped,

*A voluntary scheme, War Comforts Fund Association
(popularly Warco), expended by the end of the war
£88,794 in more than 14,000 cases of air-raid and other
distress. It gave 211,500 woollen comforts to the Forces
and £5,500-worth of cigarettes to prisoners of war.*

buses with domed tops to clear the tunnels,
and reinforced tyres to stand the continuous
scraping against the side of the kerb. These
had to be used for ordinary shuttle service
work.

The District Superintendent had eight or
nine inspectors posted at strategic points
throughout the City to give him the latest
information as to bomb craters, dangerous
structures, fire and other obstacles to the
smooth running of the omnibuses. One of
them, telephoning the result of his reconnaissance, said confidentially, 'Guv'nor, there's
been nothing like this since the fires of 1666.'
Nor had there been, but he said it with such
sincerity that the superintendent—at the
other end of the line—could not help laugh-
ing. It sounded just as though the inspector
had been present himself at the Great Fire,
and was speaking from personal recollection.

Several hundred buses, which would normally have been plying through the City at
the rate of 240 an hour, had to be diverted or
shuttled. Thus, Leyton buses went as far as
Liverpool Street and then turned round.
Camberwell buses went as far as London
Bridge before shuttling back. The question
was how many services could be maintained
without choking the roads.

The most peculiar diversion was that of the
No. 11 buses on the section of the road from
Ludgate Circus to Liverpool Street. They
had to go by the east side of St. Paul's, St.
Martin's-le-Grand, Gresham Street and Loth-
bury, and their return journey was routed
by Bartholomew Lane, Lothbury, Gresham
Street, Old Jewry, Poultry, Queen Street,
Queen Victoria Street, Blackfriars, New
Bridge Street and Ludgate Circus.

Special services had also to be arranged for
railway passengers awaiting transport at
Cannon Street. As many as twelve thousand
waited to be taken away by this emergency
service and there were still hundreds of them
queueing up when the sirens were already
wailing.

Trams, of course, could not be diverted for

obvious reasons, and it has already been shown that the smallest diversions of trolleybuses involved an immense amount of improvisations. It was therefore decided, after the air raid of December 29/30, 1940, that men would have to be detailed to the job of pulling down dangerous structures which were preventing the trams and trolleybuses from traversing their usual routes because the A.R.P. officials had not men available to pull them down. Permission was obtained from the Borough Engineers and Surveyors, and it was arranged that the tramway breakdown gangs should demolish unsafe buildings on both sides of the road to enable the tram and trolleybus services to be maintained.

An entirely new technique had to be evolved to achieve this. Two tons of steel hawser had already been purchased to meet such a contingency. This was cut into lengths of sixty and eighty feet, shackled and attached to 80-h.p. lorries with a specially low first gear. When a light loop of rope had been thrown over the highest part—usually a chimney stack—of the selected building and the steel hawser attached to it had been pulled into position, the lorry drove away in the opposite direction. Sometimes the first powerful tug would bring the top storey, or even the whole edifice, crashing to the ground. Sometimes, as in the case of a building in Gray's Inn Road, a number of violent tugs were necessary before the swaying building collapsed. Very soon the men learned the trick of an extra, final tug as the building swayed towards them.

It was risky work. The lorries and their crews were seldom more than a hundred feet from the toppling edifice, but they were cheered, both literally and metaphorically, by the crowds which collected to enjoy the sound of the crashing masonry. It was not the duty of these breakdown gangs to remove the debris once they had successfully pulled a building down. It was their business, as soon as this had occurred, to pull down the next one. In this way a whole street would be cleared in a day.

Altogether, four hundred buildings were pulled down in this manner, the most difficult job being in Charterhouse Street where a seven-floored lift-shaft had to be demolished before the City of London Engineer would give permission for the carriageway to be opened. The gangs began to pull at 5.30 p.m. The skeleton buildings, which had been burnt out, were made of steel girders, and it took two and a half hours hard work before the job was completed. As a result of this, however, the normal operation of services began in time for the first trolleybus on the following morning.

The Holborn Loop, Old Street, City Road, Theobalds Road and Hoe Street, Walthamstow, were among the other tough nuts to be literally cracked.

Omnibus diversions in the W.1 and S.W.1 districts were not quite so difficult to organise as those in the City. When Oxford Street was out of action, Wigmore Street could usually

Looking for the weakest link. Chains are used for towing for cranes and, during the war, for demolitions. Each link has to be inspected for wear and distortion. This is another example of a heavy and exacting job that was cheerfully undertaken by women.

The road spotters looked for trouble and pointed it out to the drivers.

bilities was the organising of omnibuses which would take passengers, stranded at Piccadilly Circus by the closing of the flood-gates to Waterloo, over Westminster Bridge, while a similar service of *Alert* buses were kept in readiness for the reverse journey from Elephant. At first these *Alert* buses were at Chalk Farm and Old Kent Road respectively. Later on they were parked in Jermyn Street and at Elephant itself, ready to take passengers at an instant's notice.

Later on, he organised the inter-station service which helped stranded troops and civilians to get across London during the acute shortage of taxicabs. Volunteers were called for this particularly dangerous job—all railway stations being priority targets for the Luftwaffe—and were always forthcoming.

The railway service of buses—to take railway passengers by road between sections of the line affected by the blitz—was a major headache. Urgent requests from the suburban sections of the four Main Line Railways called for a continuous stream of omnibuses which were already in short supply. It meant the milking of the regular services in order to help stranded rail passengers.

be used. When Baker Street was impassable, Gloucester Place provided a ready alternative. On some occasion or another, however, practically every side street and even alleyways in the West End were used. When Shaftesbury Avenue was out of commission, the red omnibuses rumbled round Soho Square and even through Berwick Market.

Twenty-four inspectors were posted at strategic points like Hyde Park Corner, Piccadilly Circus, Marble Arch and Baker Street, to warn the Superintendent in charge of West End buses instantly of any incident which would affect his vehicles. Sometimes the police telephoned to the Superintendent's offices at Victoria Station before the inspectors—of whom, by a miracle, only one was injured throughout the blitz.

On one occasion the inspectors had to take off their jackets and clear almost the whole length of Vauxhall Bridge Road of debris sufficiently to permit of a channel for the buses trapped in the garage near Victoria Station. As in the case of the City, the diversions ate up enormous amounts of petrol.

Another of the Superintendent's responsi-

The inter-station bus—a peacetime facility that came back for the wartime traveller.

10 The Battle of London (ii) Below Ground

ONLY MINOR damage was caused during the first ten days of January, 1941. Then came the vicious attack of January 11. The Board reported as follows:

'During the Saturday night raid, Green Park, St. Pauls, Baker Street and Bank Stations were damaged, the latter station being severely damaged. There were fatal casualties at these stations both to staff and the members of the public, but the details of these casualties are not yet available. It is practicable to use the stations for traffic as the damage does not interfere with the running of trains, but it has been necessary to close Hyde Park Corner Station owing to an unexploded bomb in the vicinity, which has also necessitated the closing of the running tunnels.

'In addition there were intermittent interruptions of the train services, particularly on Saturday night, due to incendiary and H.E. bombs, but the services were generally restored within a comparatively short while.

'On the roads on Saturday night, fifteen central buses were damaged, four of them severely; these four buses were in Bishopsgate; two drivers and one conductor were killed and one driver and two conductors injured and, as far as is at present known, twenty-two passengers were killed and others injured. The remaining eleven buses sustained minor damage, mainly broken windows, and in these incidents one driver and two conductors sustained minor injury.

'Also on Saturday night, the upper saloon of one tram at Brockley was burnt out by an incendiary bomb and one other tram and two trolleybuses had windows blown out. Elephant & Castle Tramway Substation suffered damage to the roof and windows, but there was no interference with current supply, and at Brixton Tramway Substation there was a slight fire which caused a failure of current for about an hour. On Sunday night, three trolleybuses sustained minor damage, mainly to windows, and two conductors were slightly injured.

'The position upon the road services is, of course, rather worse, particularly in the City area, although the opening of Blackfriars Bridge and Bishopsgate this morning had somewhat improved the position for the bus services; the closing of Knightsbridge is affecting West End services. On the trams there are a number of cases where the services have been broken due to track damage at Brixton Hill, at Blackfriars, in Old Kent Road and St. George's Road; an unexploded bomb in Brighton Road, Croydon, has caused a break in the through tram services and in a number of other instances overhead tram and trolleybus wires were brought down but have been replaced.

'The number of buses provided this morning for special services is 228, additional vehicles having been provided to meet the closing of the Piccadilly Line and for the replacement of services upon the Southern, and London, Midland and Scottish Railway.

'The flood-gates on the under-river sections were closed at 6.20 p.m. on Saturday and reopened at 11.39 p.m. and closed on Sunday at 6.29 p.m. and reopened at 10.52 p.m.

'The number of shelterers in the Tube stations on Saturday night was roundly 97,000 and on Sunday night 91,100; it was necessary to evacuate the shelterers from Hyde Park Corner Station on Saturday night, and these shelterers were transferred to other stations.'

The worst incident of the night occurred at the Bank Station where a bomb caused the entire roadway to collapse into the subway tunnel while the blast went down the escalators which had collapsed like a pack of cards. All the lights had gone out immediately. A rescue party from Liverpool Street found a terrible scene. There were a number of injured people by the signal cabin. There was no illumination except for the oil lamps, hand-lamps and candles carried by the rescue party.

The injured were tended and removed by ambulances which arrived in a quarter of an hour. The doctors mainly came from Bart's and worked like Trojans. The dead were left on one side—nothing could be done about them. Some of the corpses were crushed, some killed by blast, some very much mangled. Several of the shelterers had been blown on the track by the blast. A train had been actually entering when the bomb fell. It was already half-way along the platform. The blast blew the driver's hands off the controls, but the automatic brake came into action. The train stopped, but not before some of the people, blown off the platform, had been run over.

On 125 scattered acres (land owned in connection with proposed Underground extensions and the like) London Transport took to farming, producing hundreds of tons of vegetables for its 150 canteens. Hay from railway embankments went to the farm for winter horse-fodder.

The survivors made their way by the tunnel as there was no other way out. Among the casualties was a policeman going off duty and a soldier who was coming down the escalator. His rifle was blasted, stock and barrel looking like a walking stick. His uniform was burned by blast, which had also torn the clothing off other victims and badly charred their bodies.

After two or three hours the whole station had been cleared of dead and injured, except for a number of bodies ultimately recovered from beneath the escalators. A porter and ticket-collector were blown clean out of the crater by some freak of the blast. One was found wandering round, his mind a complete blank, in the early hours of the morning, and taken to Bart's.

As in the case of the Balham incident, an omnibus was in the immediate neighbourhood of the bomb. Here is the story of the driver:

'I was driving on the 21 route at the time, from Turnpike Lane to Sidcup right through the City. I was at the Yorkshire Grey public-house when the sirens sounded, and a few minutes afterwards the fun began. I journeyed on to Sidcup and in the meantime things got rough. We reached the garage and stayed there for about ten minutes. Whilst there we could hear the German bombers coming in, and we decided to clear out.

'On this occasion we worked the bus in the usual way, with a very few people on board until we got to the Old Kent Road. We then seemed to be the only moving vehicle on the road, and there was a rush for our bus from other stationary vehicles. I picked up many A.F.S. personnel, policemen and others, and carried on the journey to Tower Bridge Road.

'By that time things were getting really naughty. But we managed to continue, and got as far as King William Street, when I suddenly saw a cloud of dust and smoke, heard a terrific crash, and then I saw in front of me a big crater, and felt the bus sink beneath me. I had immediately applied my brakes, but it happened so suddenly I wondered what to do.

'I looked round and saw my conductor was still O.K. The next person I saw was a soldier, and he and my conductor with others formed a chain and helped me out of my cabin. The front of the bus was hanging over the crater, and had a broken axle. I have since learned that 111 people were killed in the shelter under the roadway where the bomb fell.

'Whilst standing there another stick of bombs fell and we lay in the gutter for a few minutes. I realised I could do nothing with the bus, it was not very "healthy" up above, so I decided to go down the nearest Tube station and 'phone my controller. I did so, and then my conductor and I made our way as best we could back to the garage where we made out an occurrence report—"Breakdown owing to enemy action".'

That same night the Superintendent in charge of City buses was on the job as usual. At Bishopsgate he saw two buildings on fire with one omnibus thrown bodily on to the pavement, and blocking the side entrance to the police station. Another bus was covered with debris. Two others had disintegrated thirty yards away. Over forty corpses were splayed all over the road and pavement. Severed arms and legs could be dimly discerned by the light of the flickering flames. Later he had to cross London Bridge whilst the blitz was still at its height, and felt very naked, with shells bursting, bombs dropping, and no protection. He had served in the Royal Horse Guards in World War I and had never experienced anything so unnerving in the whole of his army career.

There was a welcome respite for some days after the hectic night of January 11, except for a near miss on Lambeth North Station where twenty shelterers were injured and removed to hospital. This incident occurred on January 16, the date on which the Bakerloo Line terminated at Piccadilly and a special bus service to cover the break was provided to Elephant & Castle.

Bomb damage continued sporadically until the night of April 16/17. On that occasion the District Line was closed between Mansion House and St. James Park, the Bakerloo Line between Waterloo and Piccadilly Circus, the Northern Line between Strand and Kennington, the Metropolitan Line between Kings Cross and Aldersgate and between South Kensington and Edgware Road. An unexploded parachute mine was caught in the roof of Charing Cross Southern Railway Station. Blast damage was caused at Mark

Lane, Oval, West Brompton, Marble Arch, High Street Kensington, Mansion House, Kings Cross, West Hampstead, Elephant & Castle, Warren Street, Holborn and White-chapel.

The Victoria bus garage received a near miss which badly damaged ten buses, wrecked two and broke the windows of over ninety.

Three nights later there was another severe blitz. The District Line was suspended between Mansion House and Whitechapel, the Central Line between Wood Lane and Ealing Broadway, and the East London Line between Shoreditch and Surrey Docks, while bomb damage near Highgate Station neces-sitated a 15 m.p.h. speed limit on the North-ern Line. At the East Ham railway depot a land mine damaged seventy cars of the Metro-politan and District Line rolling-stock by blast.

The numbers of shelterers, which had shrunk a week previously to 50,000, promptly doubled, shrinking again to 70,000 by the notorious night of May 10. This was the worst night ever experienced by the Board. A hasty survey of the Board's railway services showed that the following damage occurred between midnight and 3.20 a.m.

00.10   55 Broadway. Portion of old building dam-aged by incendiaries. Lighting and tele-phone failed.

00.10   St. James Park—Victoria. Bomb through tunnel—feeder cables severed. Service sus-pended St. James Park/South Kensington until commencement of traffic 21.5.41.

01.00   Kings Cross. Bomb through tunnel—arch badly damaged. Train damaged and Cir-cle Lines blocked by debris—service sus-pended Baker Street/Kings Cross until 21.7.41 and Euston Square/Kings Cross until 4.10.41.

01.25   Victoria. UXB outside station. Station closed seven days.

01.30   London Road Depot. Bomb on depot—five trains damaged.

01.35   Moorgate. UXB outside station. Station closed until 08.40 hours, 13.5.41.

01.35   Aldgate. Bomb between Nos. 2 and 3 roads. Station closed eleven days.

01.45   Rotherhithe—Surrey Docks. Stations dam-aged and tunnel pierced. Service suspended until 8.6.41.

01.46   Hammersmith. Bomb adjacent to track near station. Tracks and signals damaged.

01.54   Victoria—Sloane Square. Debris on track blocking both roads (see also 00.10 hours).

01.57   Baker Street. Bomb between Nos. 3 and 4 roads. Two trains damaged. Service cur-tailed one day. Track restored 12.5.41.

02.02   Great Portland Street. Station roof damaged by blast.

02.23   Elephant & Castle. Top station damaged.

03.20   Mark Lane—Aldgate. Tunnel pierced near Tower Hill Substation. Debris on track. Service suspended Whitechapel/Charing Cross until 22.45 hours, 14.5.41.

03.20   Stepney Green. Retaining wall and staircase demolished—debris on track. Service sus-pended Bow Road/Whitechapel until 21.30 hours, 12.5.41.

All this meant that huge sections of the lines were closed. As for the buses, hundreds were damaged and the closing of Vauxhall Bridge, Oxford Circus, most of Park Lane and all the approaches south of the river to Tower Bridge, London Bridge, Southwark Bridge, Blackfriars Bridge and Waterloo Bridge, made road transport almost impossible. The trams and trolleybuses suffered at least as severely as the buses. Tram drivers, incident-ally, preferred their job to that of driving omnibuses or trolleybuses because they said that the clanging sound of the trams pre-vented them hearing approaching bombs, for by now they had become quite fatalistic.

A complete book could be filled with sur-vivors' stories of this terrible night. Here is a story of the incident at Baker Street as told by one of the Board's guards.

'I had just sat down to supper and was eating it when the inspector on duty rushed in the guards' room and said incendiaries had been dropped on Nos. 2 and 3 roads. This was about 11.0 p.m. The raid had been going on for about one hour.

'I and the others left our food and ran out of the room and over the rails to No. 3 platform. There I got sand in a bucket and ran with it towards the nearest man, who was on the line putting them out. I went backwards and forwards a few times with sand until every one was out. Then I went back to finish my supper but found it was spoilt and the tea cold.

'A little while afterwards somebody shouted, "Fire

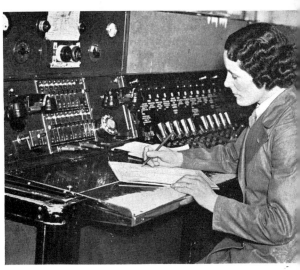

'The women who, without experience of the Board's work, left their normal occupation or . . . homes to join London Transport . . . released many thousands for the Forces and helped to maintain the services in a manner that earned the respect and admiration both of the Board and of the public.'—From the Twelfth Annual Report, December, 1945.

on No. 4 platform". I rushed out of the room again and ran across the rails of Nos. 2 and 3 roads and saw flames coming from the inside of a train that was standing on No. 4 platform. The cushions were alight.

'When I got over near it, I saw men throwing water on it, so I grabbed two buckets and ran with them to the staff lavatory where there was a tap, filled up my buckets and ran back with them to No. 4 platform, handed each to the men who were putting out the flames. How many times I went back and forth with those buckets I cannot tell, but I know that the fire was got under control; others were running back and forth with buckets of water beside me.

'After that I remember being sent upstairs with some sand. They had sent word from upstairs that they wanted more sand as the other had been used on incendiaries that had been dropped outside.

'I walked up the main-entrance stairs and a sight met my eyes over in the distance. It was as bright as day. The sky was a deep red from the fires that burned. There was the smell of burnt wood in the air, which made the eyes smart. Then would come a slight thud as they landed away in the distance. Other chaps beside myself were up there. They had been putting out incendiaries which had dropped outside on the drive and roadway.

'I was looking towards a fire that was burning on the top storeys of Bickenhall Mansions, when I heard a whistle getting nearer, and one of the chaps up there shouted, "Look out, bomb coming down". I and the others turned and ran down the stairs as quick as we could.

'I noticed that the others had dropped behind some ticket-machines that were there, but I was slow as I was looking for a place to shelter when the bang came. My ears seemed to be bursting and it felt like a hot wind going by my face. Then something seemed to be tugging at me; then I dropped flat on the floor. A glass window fell with a crash not very far from me. The lights went out, then up again; dust came down in clouds as I lay there.

'I remember I lay there for some seconds wondering what had happened. I got up and had a look round; the others behind the machines were getting up as well and looking about them. It was then that I heard rushing water coming from No. 4 platform. One of the fellows said, "That was a big one". Dust still hung in the air as I walked through the gates to go downstairs to report myself. A check had been made whilst I was upstairs and I had been missing.

'I think after that I had a walk up the platform to see if I could see where it had dropped, but I never got there for a shout came, "Fire in the offices". I ran back towards No. 5 platform stairs, but as I got there the other chaps had got fire-extinguishers in their hands and were running up the stairs to put the fire out. I know somebody shouted

to me, "Find more fire extinguishers", so I rushed round to places where they were kept but they had been used. I did find one that was full, but by the time I had found it the fire had been put out.

'I think after that I stood near the stationmaster's office and kept walking up and down Nos. 1 and 2 platforms in case any more incendiaries came down. As I looked from No. 2 platform, I saw fires burning in houses just across from the station, and as they burned they lit up Baker Street Station. Whilst standing near the stationmaster's office I heard five thuds not very far off as bombs hit the ground, and the ground shook underfoot.

'I was glad when it became light, but the *All Clear* did not go up until about 6 o'clock. Before that went, and while the guns were still firing, I went upstairs to see if any help was wanted. When I got to the main booking-hall . . . what a mess. Glass and wood-work all over the place, and dust. I've never seen such a lot before. Permanent way men were clearing wood and glass away from Nos. 3 and 4 platforms stairs so I went to give a hand, also sweeping up the booking hall as well. By then it was nearly all cleared, so I went back to the guards' room to have a brush and clean up.

'I never want another night as that.'

Now listen to what a bus driver has to say:

'It was the only night I was unable to get through to Oxford Circus. The whole of the West End was ablaze with fires and lit up like fairyland. I had to turn back at Austin Reed's. I swung my bus round in the middle of the road by Princes Garage and proceeded to go back. I was travelling towards Lambeth North Station, and just as I was about to go under Waterloo Arch, Morley College was struck. It was about two to three hundred yards away. Everything went black and my bus swayed; the first thing I did was automatically to swerve round. I managed to continue and turn into Kennington Road and pull up, and then I found I could neither go forward nor back. Eventually the road was cleared of some of the debris and we managed to carry on our journey.

'We were the last bus back. The buses were being re-fuelled and parked in the garage, and I said to the general hand on duty, "It seems a shame, all those buses should be left there. It only wants one on here and it would be a complete loss." That same night about eight bombs dropped in the locality. It was the only night I could not rest; I ate my supper standing up I was so worried. So much so did I have a kind of premonition, that I took off the suit I was wearing, it being new, and dressed in an old suit. I put the new one down the shelter for safety.

'Usually when I went on duty I always knew I was going out and coming back home safely. On this particular night, after we heard the bombs fall, I said to my wife "Something has happened at the garage, I must go round there". I live about four or five minutes' walk away from the garage, and it was then about five to three in the morning.

'Four bombs had then fallen—two of them on our garage—it was a raging furnace. I looked at the buses and the garage, and grabbed all the time cards from the lockers and put them in my pocket as I thought a roll-call would be needed, and then I thought to myself, "The best thing to do is to save some buses". There was no one else about at the time.

'I ran one bus out and put it in the road. The next one I found locked and had to leave it. I got all the front line out, then I came to the 'V'-van—there was no ignition key and, having changed my suit, my own key was in my other pocket. I began to push it out, and by that time two other people came to help me push it, including a charge hand. Suddenly a tyre burst and the charge hand flung himself flat on the ground, thinking it was a bomb!

'The next row of buses were all alight at the rear, and by that time the fire brigade had arrived and began playing a hose on the third row. I then went round to the rear of the yard and proceeded to get the buses and, I think, seven coaches. By then the fire brigade was holding the fire in check.

'There were about 110 vehicles in the garage at the time, and 74 were a complete loss. I personally drove out about five buses and the van, and assisted another fellow with others—he flooded the buses while I drove and then I flooded others while he drove them.

'We had to take a pick and shovel to get it clear for the coaches to be got out. All were got out and whilst the roof was flying, it being of asbestos. And tyres were bursting all around. The oil and differentials were going like a battlefield. The smoke and heat were terrific. We found one fellow, apparently a garage hand, who had only started work at that garage that day, lying roasted. He had apparently been knocked out by blast, pinned down by debris, and burnt alive whilst unconscious.'

When the yardmaster at Elephant & Castle ascended to ground level that night, to see what was happening, a terrible sight met his gaze. Every building in the neighbourhood was a mass of flames and it seemed highly probable that they would envelop the station. He therefore collected five members of his staff, and appealed for volunteers among the male shelterers. To his astonishment, only one warden and an old man of sixty agreed to help. But let the yardmaster tell his own story:

'I then went up to the top station again, got stirrup pumps and pails to work, fixed up the main fire hydrants in the booking-hall and on the staircase,

and had hoses run out on to the roof of the booking-hall. I called out, "Turn the cocks on", but to our dismay not a trickle of water came, as the mains had been blown up in the street.

'Knowing we had a very large storage tank at the top of the building, feeding a tap in the booking hall, six of us made up a chain gang, up the stairs and through a window on to the flat roof, throwing hundreds of pails of water on to the premises all around the station. The heat was terrific and panes of glass were falling out of the windows overhead, from premises over the station which were let out as workrooms and offices.

'Anyway, we stuck it, bombs falling and incendiaries all over the place, and the fires began to creep nearer to the booking office and substation. Suddenly a restaurant caught ablaze at the back of the booking office, and I knew what to expect. As the fire got nearer to the kitchens it was one terrific blaze, and we began to think our work was all in vain, but still we stuck it. Looking upwards we found the air shaft that ventilates the substation was getting alight, so we had to tackle that with stirrup pumps.

'We got that under control, and then the third floor occupied by a firm of milliners caught fire. We dashed up the stairs and broke down a door on the landing, and tackled this with stirrup pumps. I can well remember having to bring the water up from somewhere down at the front entrance to these premises, but I cannot recall just where we got it.

Out of a total of 1,150 porters on the Underground, 950 were women.

The Lost Property Office mirrors the fashion and accoutrement of the travelling public. Transition from 1938-1940—

'Some N.F.S. arrived but did not stop long as they could see we were getting this fire under control, and they faded away to have a go at other premises. We removed some valuable rolls of cloth and threw them out on to the landing to try and save the material. Then another fire broke out at the top of the next floor, but this did not amount to much as we caught it in time.

"All the time I had one dread—that something would get going on the main roof of the building. All on one side of this there is no protection whatever, only a step off into space from the roof, with a five-floor drop. I did not relish the thought of anyone having to go up on to the top roof, especially during the night, but I did not mention this to anyone of my company. Still, I don't think there would have been any hesitation on their part, if it had been a case of having to do it. I must say this about them all, they were the finest set of chaps that I have ever worked with under such conditions.

'I remember quite well during the course of the night that the scarf of one of the drivers caught fire. That shows how near we were working with the fire around us.

'Someone spotted that incendiaries had disappeared in the information booth outside the station entrance, and this same driver, being on the tall side, soon dealt with this.

'During another incident, we were throwing pails of water on to next-door premises when at about 3.20 a.m. we heard some whistling bombs coming

and machines roaring overhead. Someone said, "Run for it", and I can recall us scrambling through the landing window and down the stairs, in case they were meant for us. But as to getting a direct hit at any time—I think we did have the luck that night (plenty of "nears", but not one with our name on it).

'Anyway, we had done our best throughout this lot during the night, and things were still far from rosy as the fires were still going hard. I began to get a bit worried about the Board's money that was in the booking-office safe, and also about a lot of cloakroom deposits, as the walls of the booking-office and the roof were being seriously threatened. Seeing I held the keys, I decided I would save what I could.

'I took one of the men into my confidence and, together, we emptied the safe and took the books from the office and put it all under lock and key downstairs. Then we took out other things such as cloakroom-deposits, and put them into a lift that was not being used.

'Next I thought about the other station across the road, which is also under my control. I had had no time previous to this to think much about it as our time was occupied on the Bakerloo side. I left four other persons in charge, and the driver and I went over to the other station to see what had been going on.

'Things were pretty hot over there too—one seething mass of fire all around—but luck was in with the station. Some incendiaries had fallen on to the canopy roof and started a fire, but this had been dealt with by a collector. According to his account, he had had a very hectic time too.

'I decided to do the same with this booking-office money as I had done on the Bakerloo side, that was, to put it under lock and key. The driver and myself had done this and were standing in the booking-hall, when all of a sudden another bomb dropped, and the blast blew doors and windows out and sent us ducking for cover.

'Home Guards were about in the street on account of some looting that was started by some of the rough element in the neighbourhood. Having a fair amount of money from the booking-office, we decided to go by Underground to our station, as things were a bit too hot outside, what with fire engines, ambulances and hoses over the streets, and emergency water dams being fixed up in the street so that a hose could be laid along the Causeway.

'When we went up again on the Bakerloo side we did not know whether dawn had come or not, on account of the dense smoke that was about. Soon after this the sirens went for the *All Clear* and this was given to the people sheltering down below. Even now I can see the look of amazement on their faces as they made their way out of the station and saw the amount of destruction that had taken place during the night, whilst they had been down below safe and sound.'

Now for a survivor's story of the incident at Aldgate Station:

'I was driving a train on the Circle Line and we received the "red" at Notting Hill Gate. Then we carried on right the way round the Circle. We had had gunfire at South Kensington. When we got to Kings Cross I started to leave, but the "advance" signal went against me. I couldn't stop in time and I got tripped. I got down and set the trip. We stood then just by the new box. I inquired of the signalman if everything was all right. He said he would find out. He asked Farringdon who said that nothing had happened so far as they knew. I proceeded to Farringdon and found everything all right.

'When we got to Moorgate Street we had a bit of a fright. Two bombs came over whilst we were standing there. Then we got to Aldgate. We had another trip to do then. We didn't get the signal for the bay road. The signalman said we couldn't go round, and that we must stay there.

'We pulled into Aldgate. There was terrific gunfire and bombs bursting. Showers of incendiaries were coming down. I was about two coaches length away when the bomb fell. We were standing on the platform with my train beside me. The bomb smashed my cabin.

'The only effect I felt was in my ears. I seemed to go temporarily deaf, but it passed off quickly. It left a ringing in my ears which lasted for a month afterwards. My guard and I were just the same. There was a continual ringing in the ears all the time.

'In the front of the train it took all the frames and windows inside the coach, and all the seats were higgledy-piggledy. But at the other end the glass went on the platform.

'We had three men passengers who had had a few drinks. They were awkward drunks and we tried to send them out of the way but they wouldn't have any of it. They would stay with us; they felt safer. Incendiaries fell on the bridge and we helped to put them out. One drunk helped us to put them out and he made a good job of it. After the H.E. bombs dropped we never saw any more of them. I think it put the wind up them and they cleared off.

'There was terrific gunfire and bombing after that. There is a seed warehouse by the side of Aldgate Station at the end of No. 4 platform, and we watched the incendiaries fall on the warehouse and burn it out completely.

'I was saying to myself that I didn't think I would get home in the morning. I felt it was my last time. I made up my mind I was fated. It seemed so terrific. When I was driving my train round the Circle I did one and a half circuits after I had the "red" and I seemed to have that sort of fear of the tunnel—of something coming through the tunnel—because if it did you wouldn't have an earthly chance; if you weren't killed, the bomb blast would kill you. I just

—was the transition from suitcase to gas-mask case, from umbrella to rifle.

carried on, though. But I don't feel so confident now as I did.'

Now another story by a signalman, about the incident at Kings Cross:

'This particular night we were waiting in the temporary signal cabin; we had lost our signal cabin at Kings Cross by bombing. Only the lineman and myself were there; we were practically isolated from everyone. He had just left me and I was in the signal box alone. The bombs were coming down, you could almost feel the wind pressure of the H.E.'s. I remember it seemed as if there was a terrible rush of wind. I stood over the levers and put my fingers in my ears. I remember feeling a rush of wind, and when I woke up I was lying down on the floor.

'All the telephones were ringing. I thought perhaps I had fallen asleep. I was about seventy-five yards from where the bomb fell. All the lights in the signal box were out, my diagram was out and the place was choked with dust. It was just like a sandstorm. I have been out in the East.

'I rang the Controller and told him there was some trouble. The cabin was blasted and the table was turned upside down. The lineman was on the other side of the platform and was shouting to me, "Are you all right?"

'I had a look round. There was one big building left standing from the previous bomb and that had come down across the four tracks. My first thought was that I had a train standing in the tunnel. We were dealing with goods traffic. I thought about this train. I knew the guard would be nearer to the blast than me, and if I had felt it, so would he. I rang the Controller again and said I was rather anxious about the guard. He asked me if I would be good enough to see if I could find him, but not to take any risks. The lineman and myself and a ganger put on our steel helmets and went to find the guard. We found him. He said the bomb had thrown him across the brake.

'It certainly was a rough night. The others asked me what I was going to do, whether I was going to stay on the job or get out. I said, "We might walk into worse trouble. The job's here, let's stay here. It can't get any worse than this." So we stayed on the job.'

11 *If they Invade: Plan for Exodus*

MANY WEEKS of hard work passed before the services could be regarded as normal once more. Since September, 1940, a quarter of a million bombs had been dropped in Great Britain, of which a high proportion had landed in the Greater London area. On an average, eighty-four unexploded bombs were found daily.

But let some of the other men tell in their own words something of the trials of those nights and days.

A confession of faith:

'I never believed in packing up a bus, as I considered it was in Mr. Hitler's favour to do so. In driving a bus for the public, I always considered I had a weapon of war in my hand, and it was up to me to use it to advantage against the enemy.'

A psychological truth:

'Strangely enough, it seemed that people felt safe when travelling on a bus, and had every confidence in the driver, and it helped us considerably to keep going when we continually got a "Good-night, driver, and thank you".'

A bus conductor:

'At times I collected what fares I could manage, as we were only too pleased to justify ourselves being out on the road.'

A clippie:

'One night we were late turn, and the sirens went and I lost my nerve and said to my driver, "I'm not going". There was a crowd of women and children on the bus, and one woman said "Ain't you going? What about all of us?" We went as far as Old Street and then the *All Clear* went. The moment I started my fear left me.'

A guard:

'After night in and night out you get acclimatised. I felt very jumpy during the last small blitz. During the blitz a bomb dropped three doors away and blew me out of bed. On the job I am not worried, but I am when I am indoors.'

A telephone operator:

'When an alarm happened there were a lot of incoming calls, mostly inquiries from passengers, inquiries about trains and lost property. We were busy all the time. None of us were particularly worried. We just got on with the work and slept here afterwards if the raid was on.'

A tram driver:

'I think the public were served very well during the blitz. I do not think they realised it. There is a bad feeling in driving a tram. But there is an advantage in driving a tram rather than a bus. You can't hear a bomb coming or an aeroplane overhead. You don't know anything about what's happening. All you can hear is the tram going along.'

Now the threat of invasion loomed once again and highly intricate schemes were drawn up for the evacuation of refugees from the Eastern Counties. At least five thousand, mostly on foot, were expected to arrive on the north-eastern boundary of the London Civil Defence Region, where it was planned to shepherd them in the direction of Abridge, Chigwell and Woodford Bridge. Arrangements were made to move them by omnibus to billeting points in Walthamstow, Wanstead, Leyton, Hackney and Stoke Newington. Later it was decided that, in the event of invasion up the east or south-east coastal regions, this traffic would be shepherded to the roads converging on Woodford Bridge, North Kent Road and the Sanderstead Road, and it was arranged that marshalling-grounds would be established on Clapton Stadium, Charlton Football Ground and Mitcham Stadium, covering every road mentioned.

Transport arrangements were therefore revised and as a result, twenty double-deckers were earmarked for each of the three receiving depots, and a further twenty double-deckers at each of the three grounds to form a reserve if required, giving a total of 120 buses. The initial twenty buses at each depot would have been staffed on a continuous day and night basis, the necessary staff, meal relays and re-fuelling of vehicles being arranged at garages as near as possible to the receiving depots.

Roads were set aside by the Military and Police for this road refugee movement, and on the assumption that if it took place it would be of such volume that the operation of the Board's normal services on the roads concerned would be affected, provision was made for the posting of officials at critical points on the approach roads, to deal with the normal public services.

Simultaneously it was arranged with the authorities that, in the event of invasion, roads would be closed to vehicles failing to display an emergency 'E.L.' label. At the request of the War Office, too, a hundred

More than 500 officers and nearly 13,000 other ranks, including Wrens, were trained by London Transport in driving and vehicle-maintenance at Chiswick, Reigate, Northfleet and Staines.

buses were earmarked for use in an extreme emergency for the transport of troops for military purposes in the London area. This figure was later doubled.

Another important precaution was a special service to convey essential telephone-operating personnel from 21 outer-terminal points in the suburban areas to Faraday Building, Blackfriars and Victoria Station, setting down at various points along the route for other London telephone exchanges. This required 104 buses, many of which would have to do a second journey, accompanied by a G.P.O. Home Guard, in order to identify each member of the staff as they travelled from:

Sidcup	Hounslow
Bromley	Hayes
West Wickham	Harrow
Norwood Junction	Stanmore
East Croydon	Barnet
Sutton	Southgate
Kingston	Ponders End
Richmond	Walthamstow
Dagenham	Woodford
Bexleyheath	Chadwell Heath
Erith	

An earlier top secret scheme had provided for the transport from London of Govern-

ment personnel in two moves. The first, known as Black Move, was to be completed in one day and the second—Yellow Move, in two days. One thousand, six hundred and forty buses were ear-marked, each of which was to carry about 40 people and their personal luggage to the rendezvous point at Slough (Eton Playing Fields) from one or more picking-up points; the picking-up times, number of persons to be collected and arrival times at Slough being scheduled to ensure an even intake there and to avoid congestion on the routes which were specified.

On arrival at Slough personnel were to be divided into parties, according to their final destination, and again transported by a special service of buses from the Playing

Salvage often means finding a new use for an old article. Destination blinds made this part of Chiswick Works look like a nightmare travel-office.

Fields to Slough and Beaconsfield Stations to entrain for their destinations.

Buses were scheduled to arrive at Eton Playing Fields at regular intervals between 7.30 a.m. and 2.30 p.m. and Slough Station at 20-minute intervals between 10.0 a.m. and 9.20 p.m. on the Black Move; at 35-minute intervals between 10.0 a.m. and 4.30 p.m. on Day 1 of the Yellow Move, and at 30-minute intervals between 10.0 a.m. and 5.0 p.m. on Day 2. The arrival intervals at Beaconsfield Station were 60 minutes between 10.0 a.m. and 5.0 p.m. Black Move, 60 minutes between 10.0 a.m. and 5.0 p.m. Day 1 Yellow Move and not less than 90 minutes Day 2.

All persons authorised to travel were issued with identification labels and, to enable them to identify the bus by which they were to travel, all buses were to be labelled. For the guidance of each bus driver and conductor 'work tickets' giving the picking up points and times, the route to be followed and arrival times were prepared.

To avoid any delay in the timing arrangements, personnel were instructed to report at their picking-up points 15 minutes prior to the time at which they were scheduled to be picked up, and the Board's drivers and conductors were instructed to wait not more than 10 minutes after that time even if they had not their full complement of passengers. In addition, supervision was to be given by Board's officials at those points and at other selected points *en route* to Slough, and here buses were to be checked and regulated and passengers transferred, in the event of a bus arriving with a reduced number of personnel who could be accommodated on other buses, thus conserving mileage.

The supervisory arrangements to cover the control of buses and to deal with emergencies included the setting up of 13 control points and 18 regulating points with special telephone facilities and officials, including motorcyclist orderlies to maintain lines of communication between those points and with Eton Playing Fields, Slough and Beaconsfield Stations and the Board's automatic telephone exchanges at Broadway and Leicester Square. Another important feature was the engineering arrangements to deal with breakdowns. These arrangements included the provision of a 30-cwt. van with spare wheels and general spares for all types of buses, a van with a water tank, a tractor, a master lorry equipped with spares and five motor-cycle mechanics to patrol stretches of the routes to be traversed by buses.

To counteract any breakdowns between Eton Playing Fields and the entraining stations, each convoy of buses on this shuttle service was to be followed by a spare bus.

Little did the public realise the genuine menace of invasion between June, 1940, and June, 1941. It was arranged for double-deckers to be ready at six hours' notice to convey the Netherlands Ministry of Defence from the Alexandra Hotel, Hyde Park, to Worcester. Other buses were ear-marked to evacuate the *Daily Herald* staff in the early hours of the morning. Ten buses were set aside for the Regional Transport Commissioner to remove his personal staff. Another thirteen double-deckers were set aside to transport high officials from London to Stanmore, Garston and Leighton Buzzard. Yet other buses were promised to the Southern Railway to convey breakdown gangs as and when required. Another scheme was prepared for the evacuation of the Board's own garages. 'An unknown destination' was all that the Board could learn about yet another request for buses to be requisitioned by the Balloon Command of the R.A.F. One hundred and thirty buses were promised to the L.C.C. Public Health Department, to remove mental patients from any hospital damaged by enemy action. Another ninety-five double-deckers were ear-marked for the transport of twelve thousand potential refugees from Romford and Hornchurch.

Already the Lost Property Office was reflecting war conditions in its own peculiar way. The transfer of numbers of civilians to the Forces was indicated clearly enough by the much smaller number of umbrellas which were lost. Suitcases also dropped in numbers. In their place came hundreds of steel helmets—Army, Navy and Civil Defence—French steel helmets, French officers' *képis*, Land Army girls' hats and coats, war correspondents' caps, even rifles and bayonets! One wonders what excuses the neglectful warriors gave at their subsequent kit inspection.

12 Bombing diminishes: London Transport makes Munitions

GERMANY HAD now attacked Russia and the bombers which had busily been attacking London were switched to the Eastern Front, in such numbers that the Board was temporarily able to suspend its daily report to the Railway Executive Committee of incidents affecting the Board's property.

Increasing war production was bringing more and more workers to London and the need for staggering working hours became irresistible. Under statutory powers, over eleven hundred firms were brought into the scheme. Local transport groups were formed in the London area. Eventually there were fifty-five group leaders who formed local converging points for queries and complaints and the adjustments required by local and special conditions. These group leaders continuously provided information, details of changed conditions, of faults and short-comings. The co-ordinating process affected offices, schools, shops, places of entertainment and even hospital visitors. The public's co-operation was begged in every possible way, considerable success was ultimately achieved and, indeed, the process of staggering was simplicity itself. All that was required was for the factory workers and school children to start and end their day in groups divided by a mere quarter of an hour.

The following figures show the number of employees arriving at a group of factories in East London. They reveal that in sections of the peak hours, overcrowding was rampant, causing bad time-keeping and loss of 'drive', while at other times accommodation was not fully employed.

NUMBER OF WORKERS ARRIVING

a.m.	old rate (before staggering)	new rate (after staggering)
7.00	302	302
7.15	—	3,000
7.30	5,514	2,514
7.45	56	3,556
8.00	6,337	2,067
8.15	—	870
8.30	900	900

Strangely enough the difficulties of coping with the transport of war workers were increased by the Board itself. For it was already hard at work on war production which bore no parallel to its peacetime activities. Thus, though the modern heavy bomber like the Halifax is possibly the most highly developed piece of engineering yet produced, the Board undertook—without previous experience—to manufacture the centre section, to install engine units and the front fuselage, and finally, the complete erection and test-flying of Halifaxes, the other sections being undertaken by Chryslers, Duple, Express Motor & Body Works Limited, and Park Royal Coachworks. London Transport, as the co-ordinating centre of the group, received all drawings, modifications and improvements, broke them down and segregated them.

The nucleus of the organisation was established at Chiswick, but the programme required additional space, and it was decided to complete and occupy buildings then in process of construction at Aldenham on the extension of the Northern Line. London Transport was later invited to take over a new factory at Leavesden and assume responsibility for the final erection, test-flying and delivery of the complete aircraft.

The staff was drawn largely from the various engineering departments, though very few of them had any previous experience of aircraft construction. Arrangements were therefore made for visits to be made to Handley Page and a number of workers were given a chance to work for some months there. This was all the tuition available before the first machines were assembled. A large number of workers were completely inexperienced and unskilled women.

The provision and the manufacture of assembly jigs, tools and equipment was in itself a major production problem. Skilled tool makers were unobtainable and so large numbers of body makers, carpenters and pattern makers had to be trained for this highly specialised work. Standard high-precision, special engineering tools were unobtainable from the usual sources. Scarcity of machine tools made it necessary to spread the machining work over no fewer than five hundred different sub-contractors. Members of the staff had to be sent all over the country to search for any machinery capable of doing the job. It was under these conditions that the first two hundred aircraft were produced. Ultimately over seven hundred were completed.

Since the war many engineering secrets such as 'Pluto', 'Fido', and 'Mulberry' have been disclosed. Many of them were entirely novel, others embodied well-tried principles a new way, but all demonstrated British ingenuity. A first-class example of this quality was provided by the factory installed in one of the Tubes.

The selected tunnel lay between Leytonstone and Gants Hill—nearly five miles of railway tube, four yards in diameter—with three stations at Wanstead, Red Bridge and Gants Hill, giving 300,000 square feet of factory floor-space. The shape of this Wellsian factory made it evident that, to avoid long walks for the employees to their machines, there would have to be other intermediate entry points at Cambridge Park and Danehurst Gardens, in addition to the three railway stations. This was done, and no employee had more than four hundred yards to walk to his or her place of work.

*The first London Aircraft Productions Halifax was flown
in 1941. The last (the 710th), named 'London Pride',
was delivered to the R.A.F. in April, 1945.*

A miniature railway had to be built to convey the materials. Lights had to be spaced equally over the long row of machines tended by the girls in their white overalls. Special air-conditioning had to be installed. Cloakrooms had to be warmed and temperatures controlled thermostatically. First-aid rooms had to be provided with mechanical ventilation. A subterranean canteen for six hundred people, and four mess rooms capable of seating sixteen hundred were also necessary.

For the execution of many varied building operations the services of the architect, heating and lighting engineers, and the engineers of the Building Department were actively sought. To them fell the duty of providing new structures, making alterations (four aircraft factories were equipped by 'making and mending') and fitting up much of the accommodation called for by wartime conditions.

The Building Department did special work outside its normal activities. They made parts for trestle bridges, deck panels, landing-ramps; they built 55 great pontoon floats, each thirty-five feet long, eight feet wide and five feet deep. They made a tank for test-floating them.

One unusual job was the production of turntables for aircraft, the purpose of which was to carry craft so that they could be rotated for the adjustment of the magnetic instruments in all positions. No iron or steel could be used in the construction. A load of four tons had to be carried at any point on the turntable, which was thirty-six feet in diameter in the largest type; the weight was fourteen and a half tons. The job was done within seven weeks.

In common with the other sections, Charlton tram and trolleybus works turned its attention, with resounding success, to the 'extra-mural' war effort.

Ingenuity underground—the five-mile factory for aircraft components.

Charlton went in mainly for ammunition and gun parts. They turned out 2 in. Mark II H.E. shells to the tune of 158,000. And in addition to machining shafts for tank gear-boxes to the number of 16,170, they produced 37,000 blanks for Channel Grenade Dischargers, forged and machined parts for aircraft ground equipment, machined spare parts for two-pounder gun mountings and visor parts for tanks.

They machined main tubes for Stiffkey sights, blocks and brackets, universal mountings for 20 mm. guns, gland washers and components for Admiralty small guns—fifteen thousand of these—cartridge barrels and spindles for 17-pounder guns.

They made iron-castings and machined breech and mechanism levers, jigs and machine fixtures, press tools and gauges; they supplied forgings.

The Buses and Coaches Department built 897 Ford and Chevrolet lorries, twenty armoured lorries, overhauled 4,000 War

Department vehicles, made about fifty thousand sets of electrical parts for tanks, re-ground eighty crank-shafts per week for the Army, produced many varieties of sheet-metal work for the Ministry of Supply contractors, and a host of other items, besides carrying out a vast amount of repair work.

Then, in response to a request by the Minister of War Transport for ambulances for United States Forces, they stripped a hundred coaches of their seating and equipment, and converted them. These did valuable work.

Aircraft . . . torpedo sights . . . and much more. An urgent appeal was made by the Government for armoured vehicles, and for more and more facilities for the overhaul of damaged ones.

London Transport's Acton works undertook this task. The work they carried out varied from the machining of a wide range of light and medium intricate components and assembling to high precision limits, to hand forging and the construction of bodies for Army breakdown lorries.

The number of orders placed on the works approached a thousand. Searchlight lamps were called for, and spares for A.F.V. control gear, and recuperators—each consisting of many parts. Many orders necessitated the manufacture of jigs and fixtures.

Then Acton undertook further jobs; overhaul, repair and testing of landing-craft motors and generators for the Admiralty, rebuilding railway wagons for the Southern Railway. The permanent way shops began manufacturing torpedo-boat engine bases and canopies, noses for naval shells, caterpillar-frames for excavating-machines, altering and equipping tanks for the laying of bridges (these tanks had to have the turret removed and be reconstructed with mechanism to launch a bridge over gaps up to thirty feet, the bridge to be capable of carrying a fifty-ton weight). They converted tanks to operate in water up to ten feet deep off Normandy beaches and these were used on D-day.

Acton works built other kinds of vehicles than the armoured variety. They provided,

A breakdown lorry for the U.S. Army. One of 49 special bodies that were designed and built at Acton works.

(Above) *Testing a bridging pontoon.* (Below) *London Transport's own spare-time factory at Earls Court.*

for instance, three personnel coaches for Rail Mounted Artillery, saloon coaches, thirty-three Metropolitan Line coaches for Southern Command for use as hutments; to this Command they also supplied seventy-eight coach bodies.

To the Admiralty they supplied three saloon-type cars and one compartment coach complete with bogies, for the use of H.M.S. *Bee*, and two coaches for ratings' sleeping accommodation. They supplied to the Ministry of Fuel and Power, ten coaches equipped as mobile hostel units for miners. They brought out fifteen saloon-type coaches scheduled for scrapping; a firm of contractors removed the bodies and sold the underframes and bogies to Vickers-Armstrongs.

Much ingenuity was displayed in the Signal section. The department had to evolve apparatus for meeting many diverse situations. They produced warning and protective devices for the Tube flood-gates. They were authors of the bomb detector and location devices for use at the Tube under-river tunnels. Other successful innovations included the establishment of a factory where the Board's staff worked in their evenings' spare time on war work. The value of the output exceeded £200,000.

The Ventilation section had a great deal to do in connection with the ventilation for Tube railway shelters and of the various underground activities. These included staff shelters and dormitories, decentralised and other offices, control centres, auto-telephone exchanges, canteens, substations, works, underground passages for the storage of public authorities' records and treasures which housed such items as Somerset House records, British Museum treasures and valuables belonging to the Office of Works. They also provided certain accommodation for the G.P.O. and an emergency headquarters for the L.C.C. ambulance telephone exchange.

← *The Shermans arrive for overhaul at Acton.*

13 'The Land is Bright': D-day

As LONDONERS will recall, major incidents between January, 1943, and January, 1944, were pleasantly rare. The exception occurred on March 12, 1943, at Ilford Broadway when the overhead wiring was damaged by a high explosive bomb and the streets were machine-gunned. An omnibus was burnt out and the driver was burnt to death. A district inspector travelling on a trolleybus was killed by a machine-gun bullet.

Now came the 'scalded cat' raids of February and March, 1944. Once again it was necessary for the Board to make a daily report. On February 19, the overhead wires, high-tension cable, gas and water mains were damaged in Chiswick High Road and the bus and trolleybus services were interfered with for over a month. On the same day the services on the Hammersmith and City Line were suspended between Latimer Road and Hammersmith owing to bomb damage at Goldhawk Road. A bomb in the roof of Marlborough Road tunnel reduced speed on the Metropolitan Line to 10 m.p.h. between Baker Street and Finchley Road. Damaged bridges completely suspended services between Wood Lane and Ealing Broadway on the Central Line, while the Bakerloo Line trains were restricted to 10 m.p.h. between Kilburn Park and Maida Vale.

On the following day a bomb in Falcon Road near Clapham Junction damaged the overhead wires and the tram lines were out of commission for nearly three months.

A great deal of work was required during this phase to check the many reports of suspected unexploded bombs. Many of these proved to be unfounded, or concerned bombs too far from the Board's property to be of any consequence.

The Luftwaffe was using heavy phosphorus bombs as well as incendiaries. A shower of the latter at Earls Court set fire to a train near the station, temporarily blocking the track. Minor damage was also caused to Sloane Square Station (blast), to Park Royal (an incendiary bomb) and to Alperton (H.E.), but the emergency repair squads were so quickly on the job that the public scarcely knew that damage had been done.

Altogether there were sixteen incidents affecting trams caused by debris, anti-aircraft shells and phosphorus bombs; with four exceptions they were cleared within a few hours.

On the roads a number of Central bus routes had to be diverted or worked short of their terminal points. These short, sharp raids caused the number of shelterers to rise once again to the sixty thousand mark, after having dwindled to only a few thousand. . . .

D-day was now approaching and the Board official who was detailed at the end of April, 1944, to plan a series of top secret bus routes from Wanstead to the Royal Albert, the Victoria and the West India Docks, was informed that he must be available for immediate consultation from May 25. This gave him a fair indication of the proximity of the invasion date, but naturally, like other officials of the Board entrusted with vital information, he concealed all external interest in the current rumours about D-day.

Nearly three weeks were necessary for him to survey the various bus operations which, starting from Wanstead, involved transit camps as far apart as Canning Town and Purfleet. Secrecy was all important, and the highest praise must be given to the Board drivers who volunteered to work on their rest days—conveying the spearhead of the attack to the transports ultimately *en route* for Normandy.

The actual movement of the invasion troops began on June 2. Between that date and July 4, the rumbling red omnibuses of the London Passenger Transport Board conveyed infantry of no fewer than six divisions right alongside the ships and assault craft destined to make the perilous voyage across the Channel.

Nor was this operation without incident. Fifteen of the omnibuses were waiting for instructions at Snaresbrook Road, Wanstead, when a doodlebug exploded on a block of flats forty yards away, blasting them completely. By an extraordinary coincidence the bus crews were, for the first time, not playing solo in one of the omnibuses and, in consequence, no casualties were incurred, though every vehicle lost its windows and many others suffered serious damage.

A favourite recollection of the Board's official in charge of the operation concerns Purfleet. Having served in the Royal Navy in World War I, he came to the conclusion that the width of the broad arterial road would make it possible for his fleet of omnibuses—detailed to pick up the troops—to carry out a naval manoeuvre. The omnibuses having arrived from London and having filled up with 42 infantrymen apiece turned 180 deg. simultaneously in one minute, so that they were all facing in the correct direction of the embarkation points.

Incidentally, men of the Upton Park Garage from which volunteers had originally been sought, were so keen to do the job alone that there was almost a mutiny when the Board decided that they would have to share the honours with Forest Gate and Athol Street Garages.

In a very short time many of the Board's drivers had the melancholy privilege of collecting the army casualties from the hospital trains which set down stretcher cases at Tattenham Corner, Epsom Town and Addison Road. Each Green Line ambulance was able to take eight stretcher cases.

In this connection many people may wonder why Addison Road Station figured so prominently in evacuation, re-vacuation and on this occasion. The answer is that Addison Road has an unusually wide platform—ideal for handling the wounded, the crippled, pregnant mothers and infants, while the cul-de-sac road leading to it was an additional advantage. Several thousand men wounded in France were taken to military hospitals in the Board's vehicles in this way.

Over four thousand Canadian casualties were handled by six converted ambulances within ten weeks of D-day. The Canadian military reception-hospital was at Woking-ham and the casualties were brought from Ascot railway station and Wokingham rail-way station, later moving to dispersed hos-pitals as far away as Cuckfield in Sussex. Some of these converted ambulances took eighteen sitting-up cases; others carried nine or ten stretcher cases.

14 *The New Threat: V-weapons*

THE FIRST V.1 incident to affect the Board was at Grove Road, Bow, when the rail-way bridge was hit and the girders crashed into the road. Within two hours of its explo-sion at dawn, the Operating Manager of Trams and Trolleybuses was on the scene. A quick discussion with the police and Air Ministry officials informed him that the damage had been caused by 'an aeroplane which must have burst in the air'. For twenty-four hours the authorities kept a security silence on the subject of this and other myster-ious explosions. Thus, a paragraph in the report of London Transport's Chief Engineer (Civil) Department contained this para-graph:

'On Thursday, June 15, 1944, an air-raid warning was sounded at 11.37 p.m. It was reported from Kentish Town Station that a noise and a flash had been observed in the direction of Prince of Wales Road. At 11.51 p.m. the signalman at Farringdon reported that something had fallen between Farring-don and Kings Cross which was believed to be an aeroplane.'

Next day an official announcement was made to the effect that the new menace was, in fact, the flying bomb. Thenceforward *Alerts* were frequent and lengthy, and another large-scale evacuation took place. More than a quarter of a millon evacuees were taken to Main Line stations between July 5 and September 18, 1944. Ninety thousand more passengers were carried by trams and trolley-buses and on the Board's railways.

The Board's property suffered considerable damage throughout the V.1 period. Tram tracks and railways were frequently hit.

On an average twenty incidents affecting the Board's property or vehicles were re-ported every day for the next fortnight. Altogether from June 16 to August 31, there were 270 incidents, fifty-three of which caused serious damage. Battersea Garage alone suf-fered from three different doodlebugs within a fortnight. Camberwell Garage was hit four times, quite apart from the tram depot and the substation which were also hit. Elmers End Garage received a direct hit on July 18.

It was a fine summer evening, and a dozen of the staff were in the entrance to the garage, when they heard a doodlebug bumbling along. Suddenly it cut off and, worse still, it could be seen diving straight for the building.

Everyone scattered. Half of them dived for the kit room, the others for the shelter. The

Sampling their gift at the handing-over ceremony. Com-rades in the Forces were never forgotten. London Transport staff gave seven mobile canteens to the Y.M.C.A. and then paid for their maintenance.

six who went to the kit room were killed instantly. The doodlebug, crashing into and exploding against the near side of the main entrance, wrecked the traffic office, the ticket department, the canteen, the A.R.P. stores, the cleaners' room, the inside-staff mess-room, as well as the kit room.

The depot inspector was taking cash at the time from a woman conductor. Hearing the explosion he threw himself instantly to the floor, taking cover near the safes. The woman was killed. Within a few minutes the garage was alight. The N.F.S. hurriedly appeared on the scene, but one petrol tank after another of the parked buses exploded. The tyres smouldered and smelled horribly. Debris was scattered everywhere. The inspector set up an office in a damaged bus inside the nearby cemetery so that returning crews could pay in.

That night urgent telephone calls to various garages enabled the Elmers End Garage to borrow omnibuses and tickets so that next morning the run-out was exactly according to schedule—except for two buses which started a few minutes late. Admittedly the staff had to sign on at the cemetery and some of the buses were windowless, while others had no destination blinds. But the services went on, in spite of the fact that twenty-seven double-deckers, two single-deckers, and ten ambulances had been put completely out of action.

On the railways the serious incidents which appreciably affected traffic occurred at Essex Road, Ravenscourt Park, Aldersgate, Walham Green, West Brompton and South Kensington.

A bomb on the Black & White milk bar and dance-hall in Putney High Street damaged the Board's property, and within three minutes of the explosion a dozen of the Board's ambulances had arrived. Their crews hurried to the scene of death and helped to rescue hundreds of injured people, transferring them to local hospitals. Later on that night, at the request of the group ambulance officer, they removed seventy mangled corpses to Kingston Vale mortuary.

Where ignorance is bliss . . . Londoners who had recently been exhilarated by the swift fall of Paris and Brussels, though depressed by the glorious failure of Arnhem, would have been taken aback, to say the least of it, if they had known the plans for their safety being formulated by the police, the Senior Regional Officer, London, and the Regional Transport Commissioner in September, 1944.

The increasing success of the Anti-Aircraft Command in shooting down the doodlebugs suggested that the danger from them had reached its peak. But our agents on the Continent had transmitted sufficient warnings about the V.2's as to make it necessary for the sternest precautions to be taken in the event of this so-far-unknown weapon being brought into action. Coupled with this was the German threat of retaliation for our saturation bombing of German cities.

All of these pointers added up to the fact that London was likely to be subjected to mass destruction from the air, and the necessary precautions had therefore to be taken. It can now be revealed, for the first time, that the most elaborate plans were formulated by the Board for the dispersal of London refugees. It was decided that the best method of dealing with the problem was to select (with the aid of the police) suitable assembly points outside the radius of about five miles from the centre of London. At these, parties of refugees, who would have begun to make their escape on foot, would be picked up by omnibus and transported to the 'fringe' areas.

The selected picking-up points were mostly cinemas, dance halls, schools and football stadiums. The inhabitants of Sidcup, for example, had no idea that every detail had been planned for their being ordered to tramp to the Central School at Alma Road, or to the Odeon Cinema, Station Road, from where they would be driven through the blitz to Maidstone. The refugees of Beckenham, so it was planned, were to make their way to the Regal Cinema in the High Street from where they would be driven to Sevenoaks. The refugees of Bromley and Orpington would also have been instructed to meet at their local cinema or cinemas for transportation—also to Sevenoaks.

Altogether there were eighty-seven top-secret routes for refugees to the 'fringe' area. Choosing them at random one finds that among the picking-up points were Tiffin Boys' School at Kingston, Chiswick Empire at Chiswick, the Cuckoo Infants' Schools at Hanwell, the Dominion Cinema at Harrow, the Kings Hall Cinema at Penge, the Spurs Football ground at Tottenham, the Regal Cinema and the Methodist Hall at Lambeth, the Gaumont Cinema and Hall of Remembrance at Chelsea, St. Peter's School and St. Barnabas' School at Westminster, the Conway Hall and Laystall Street School at Holborn, the Grand Cinema and the L.C.C. School at Marylebone and the Regal Cinema and the Prince of Wales Cinema at Paddington.

Elmers End Garage after the V.1—and still the next morning's buses left according to schedule.

Here is the grim memorandum entitled:

REFUGEES

MOVEMENT BY ROAD TO REST CENTRES IN 'FRINGE' AREAS

1. The assembly points are situated on or near the main roads out of London and it will generally be convenient that the buses, when loaded, should proceed along the main roads on or near which they have picked up their loads. The bus drivers will have to be given specific destinations at which to report in the first instance, and for this purpose regulating stations on the main roads and on or near the inner edge of the 'fringe' area will be required.

2. Each regulating station should be so situated that the distribution of refugees among the Rest Centres along the whole length of the main road and in the areas adjoining the road can be controlled from the regulating station. The station must be close to the inner edge of the 'fringe' area so that buses taking refugees to Rest Centres near the inner edge do not have to double back after reporting.

3. Each regulating station should be manned by an officer of the Public Assistance Authority, empowered to exercise complete control over the operation of the Rest Centre Service within the area served by the station, and able to obtain prompt information about the numbers of refugees in each Rest Centre in that area. Large numbers of persons

London Transport men and women in the march-past of the public utility contingent of Civil Defence, Hyde Park, May, 1945.

will no doubt arrive in Rest Centres otherwise than by special bus transport and must be allowed for in directing the buses to their final destinations.

4. If possible, an officer of the Ministry should be at each regulating station to maintain liaison with the Public Assistance Authority, to keep an eye on the general development of the situation and to report as may be necessary to the Senior Regional Officer.

5. Special arrangements for co-ordination between Public Assistance Authorities may be necessary where a main road crosses the boundary between the areas of two such authorities. It is important that there should be no risk of disputes between authorities on the question of the fair allocation of the refugees.

6. On arrival at a regulating station, bus drivers must be given specific directions, with the least possible delay, as to the precise location of the Rest Centres at which they are to set down their loads. Each bus should, as far as possible, be directed to a single destination where the whole bus-load can be set down. If dispersal in small parties to a number of Rest Centres is necessary, this should be effected by the use of local transport.

7. Arrangement should be made for the drivers to be given a meal or at least light refreshments either at the Rest Centres or on the return journey at the regulating station.

8. Regulating stations should be selected in consultation with the Regional Transport Commissioner and the Public Assistance Authorities concerned. In considering the position of the regulating stations and the routes to be taken by buses from regulating stations to Rest Centres, regard must be had to the existence of low bridges or other obstacles to the passage of double-decked buses. On this point, the Divisional Road Engineer of the Ministry of Transport should be consulted.

9. When regulating stations have been settled, Head Office should be furnished with detailed particulars of:

   (a) The precise situation of the regulating stations.

   (b) Precise directions as to reporting at the regulating stations.

   (c) The area controlled from each station and the amount of Rest Centre and reception centre accommodation in that area.

   (d) The authority in charge of the Rest Centre arrangements in each area, with, if possible, the name of the officer responsible for the control of the operations and the address from which he will operate (with telephone number).

15 *VE-day: Putting the House in Order*

Now—with the approach of the 1944 winter—came the rockets. The first of these to affect the Board's property exploded near Walthamstow trolleybus depot. Others caused minor damage at Forest Gate and Upton Park. For some months V.1's and V.2's fell indiscriminately out of the sky, and the strain on the flood-gate control operators was very considerable.

The first tram track damage from a rocket occurred in November, 1944, when a track was cut by a crater measuring forty feet by twenty feet. Then a rocket fell in Lambeth Road.

Such was the speed with which the staff dealt with these incidents that, in the second instance, the down track was ready for service next morning. A few days later a rocket damaged the tracks in Green Lanes. The down track was ready for service within ten days. Next came a bad rocket incident in Jamaica Road. Sewer damage held up repair work for several weeks. This made three serious interruptions to tram services, all due to rockets.

Properties as well as tram tracks suffered. West Ham Depot was damaged, as was Aldersgate Station. There were incidents on the District Line west of Walham Green, and at the tunnel mouth between West Brompton and Walham Green.

Walthamstow Trolleybus Depot, Forest Gate Garage, Upton Park Garage and Norwood Depot were among other properties damaged more or less seriously. A bridge at West Hampstead Metropolitan Line Station was damaged and the tracks covered with debris. Potters Bar Garage suffered and so did Hounslow West Station.

During the whole of the attacks by rocket bombs (and by a few flying bombs interspersed amongst them) the road services suffered much less than during the main flying bomb attacks of 1944, although the staff worked for many weeks under conditions which were just as unpleasant.

In no case was a garage the subject of a direct hit, and buses in general escaped serious damage.

The two garages most seriously affected were close together, Forest Gate and Upton Park which, between them, had three rockets in the immediate vicinity within thirty-six hours. At Forest Gate the rocket fell fifty yards from the premises just after midnight, shattering the roof glasses, damaging thirty-two buses and depriving the garage of water, gas, electricity and the telephone. Fortunately there were no injuries to the staff, who at once set about clearance of buses and premises to such effect that all service buses left the garage to time, although some ran without windows. Twenty-four hours later a rocket fell within 150 yards of the same garage causing further damage to the roof, blowing the windows out of three more buses and injuring slightly one of the engineering staff.

Ten hours after Forest Gate had suffered for the second time, a rocket fell within fifty yards of Upton Park Garage in the middle of a Sunday morning, and caused extensive damage to buses parked in the garage. The garage roof lost most of its glass, while offices and workshops were damaged. Despite this the engineering staff on duty sustained only two minor casualties. In all, 134 buses and coaches were damaged; these, coupled with those previously damaged at Forest Gate, plus five others damaged by incidents while in service, caused these two garages a total of 171 damaged vehicles.

The Board's most-bombed garage, Athol Street, in Poplar, close to the Docks, suffered once more when a rocket exploded within a hundred yards of the garage at 6.0 a.m. on a Saturday morning, causing considerable damage to the roof and blowing the windows out of 25 buses, but without casualties to the staff who succeeded in the astonishing feat of getting all of the buses out of the garage on time. While repairs were being effected during the next day, another rocket exploded in the air, undoing all the work that had been done to the buses and doing considerably more damage to the roof. Two days later four pieces of another rocket, bursting near by, fell into the garage, but the only damage was to the fire-sprinkler system. As usual at this garage, the staffs worked wonderfully well and no buses were delayed.

Other garages damaged were Plumstead, Swanley and Epping, the roof glasses being broken and a certain amount of damage being done to windows and doors.

Buses were damaged at widespread points throughout the eastern, north-eastern and south-eastern districts, and occasional incidents occurred to buses in south and central London. The majority of the damage was broken windows, which were repairable at the garages, 440 vehicles being dealt with from September 12, 1944, to March 27, 1945. During the same period, fifty-six vehicles were damaged sufficiently heavily for them to be sent to Chiswick works for repairs. Most of these casualties were the result of rocket-bomb attacks, although a number were caused by flying bombs.

As during the previous enemy attacks, the maintenance staffs worked on under very difficult conditions. They could take no cover from the rocket bombs and had to work under the continuous strain imposed by the sudden explosions which they produced. Especially in the Barking, Grays, Epping, Ilford, Seven Kings, Leyton, Dalston, Poplar and Plumstead areas, life was most uncomfortable for the staffs both at home and at work. The net result of their efforts was, however, that on no occasion were insufficient buses available for service requirements.

The last London Transport incident of the war seems to have been at Whitechapel, where there was debris on the East London Line, and windows in the station and the substation roof were damaged. Traffic was interrupted for forty minutes.

At long last VE-day dawned and the evacuees started pouring back in their thousands, necessitating further work for the hard-pressed drivers and conductors of omnibuses, trams and trolleybuses. But the Board did not wait for the fall of Japan to put its house in order as quickly as possible.

For five years and more, the blast and light-trap walls had made tortuous the path of those entering and leaving Underground stations. Tooting was the first station to be relieved of its wall. Then Clapham South, and Clapham North; and at the rate of about three per day the remaining forty-eight disappeared more completely than the walls of Jericho.

At the same time there disappeared 541,922 square yards of window netting and other A.R.P. impedimenta. Large quantities of sandbags went from stations, garages, works and depots; 850 tons were cleared from one building alone.

Netting on the windows of vehicles was removed within seven weeks, to the great satisfaction of Londoners. The adhesive, a special heavy-bodied varnish, took a good

The children come back for good. In all the various evacuation schemes London Transport carried about 1¼ million persons.

In the shelters themselves, the final bunk—the last of twenty-six miles—was removed on May 31, 1945. On the same day the last of the eighty medical-aid posts was also dismantled.

By that time no fewer than 22,580 of the regular staff had been called for service in the Forces, Merchant Navy and full-time Civil Defence, while, in the air attacks on London, another 245 were killed and 1,006 injured besides those previously referred to as killed and wounded on duty. Many honours and awards were earned by members of the staff: 122 military decorations, ranging from C.B. to B.E.M., were awarded to staff serving in the Armed Forces, and one K.B., five C.B.E.s, eight O.B.E.s, ten M.B.E.s, two G.M.s, and 29 B.E.M.s were gained by those who 'carried on'.

Charles Graves

deal of removing; in many instances, the netting had been on the windows for over four years, and had not deteriorated in any way. More than 381,500 windows had to be dealt with. Many of them, which had cracked into countless fragments, had remained firmly bound together by the adhesive which had undoubtedly saved many passengers from serious injury.

One of the biggest jobs was the demolition of the sanitary equipment from Underground shelters. Another major job was the removal of 125 shelterers' canteen points, with their 450 ten-gallon electric urns.

All the other shelter obstructions and equipment on the platforms and subways were dismantled and removed in 3½ weeks. Fifteen hundred tons of material were dealt with; and no trace was left of the presence of A.R.P. equipment.

The bomb-locating devices (page 11) are taken up from the bed of the Thames. . . . . London is safe.

METRO-LAND

1932 EDITION

CONTENTS

METRO-LAND was an annual guide, first published in May 1915, that acted as a 'comprehensive description of the country districts served by the Metropolitan Railway'. It appeared until 1933, at first costing 1d, then rising by 100% to 2d! Its contents were directed at walkers, excursionists, party organisers and house hunters. The guide defined Metro-land as "the beautiful unknown country ... the rural arcadia ... close to London". It began at Wembley Park and extended out to Chesham, Brill, Verney Junction and Uxbridge. It offers brief descriptions, illustrated by photographs, of the areas around each station and an 'Historical Sketch of Metro-land'.

Available from Oldcastle Books Ltd, 18 Coleswood Rd, Harpenden, Herts, AL5 1EQ. £9-95 cloth, £5-95 paper (+£0-95 P&P).